Mary Magdalene, Bride in Exile

"Controversial and provocative. . . . Starbird puts her distinctive touch on re-examining the legacy of Mary Magdalene and reclaiming the long-exiled Lost Feminine; an insightful journey, a beacon of hope for our time."

KAREN RALLS, PH.D., AUTHOR OF
THE TEMPLARS AND THE GRAIL

"A superbly written and meticulously researched work by a scholar of great integrity. Her insight has once again made a significant contribution to my understanding."

TIM WALLACE-MURPHY, COAUTHOR OF
CUSTODIANS OF TRUTH: THE CONTINUANCE OF REX DEUS

Also by Margaret Starbird

The Goddess in the Gospels:
Reclaiming the Sacred Feminine

Magdalene's Lost Legacy:
Symbolic Numbers and the Sacred Union
in Christianity

The Woman with the Alabaster Jar:
Mary Magdalen and the Holy Grail

Mary Magdalene, Bride in Exile

MARGARET STARBIRD

Bear & Company
Rochester, Vermont

Bear & Company
One Park Street
Rochester, Vermont 05767
www.InnerTraditions.com

Bear & Company is a division of Inner Traditions International

Library of Congress Cataloging-in-Publication Data

Starbird, Margaret, 1942–
  Mary Magdalene, bride in exile / Margaret Starbird.
      p. cm.
  Includes bibliographical references and index.
  ISBN 1-59143-054-2 (pbk.)
  1. Mary Magdalene, Saint—Miscellanea. 2. Jesus Christ—Miscellanea. I. Title.

  BS2485.S686 2005
  226'.092—dc22
                                                                    2005013848

Printed and bound in the United States by Lake Book Manufacturing, Inc.

10 9 8 7 6 5 4 3 2 1

Text design and layout by Priscilla Baker
This book was typeset in Sabon, with Tagliente, Charlemagne, and Avenir used as
display typefaces

"In memory of her"

Contents

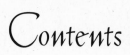

Acknowledgments

Without the loyal and unflagging support of my husband and children, I could not have taken this "path less traveled." My life's journey has not always been comfortable for them, and I thank them now for their faith in me that allowed me to make my quest. My father has always been a rock in my life, and his acceptance and encouragement of my work has been more important to me than I can ever express. I also want to thank my close friends in the prayer community Emmanuel, especially Mary Beben, Sue Gehringer, and Faye Biskup, who have continued to offer insights and suggestions in addition to their prayers over many years of spiritual kinship.

The competent support of the editors and staff at Inner Traditions, Bear and Company has been enormously helpful in my work. I especially want to thank Peri Champine for her expert help with assembling the art in this volume, Jon Graham for his assistance with art, and Elaine Cissi for her insightful editing. We are "instruments playing in a common band." I am also immensely grateful to the staff of the Grandstaff Library at Fort Lewis, Washington, for cheerfully researching my interlibrary loan requests, without which I could never have written any books, especially this one.

I want to thank Lesa Bellevie for her ongoing commitment to the www.magdalene.org Web site and community e-mail list letter that she so generously supports and moderates, a forum that has made huge contributions to research of Mary Magdalene and her manifestation in consciousness. I am particularly indebted to Lesa for sharing insights about the "Bride in Exile," a phrase that so beautifully expresses the lost bride of the Christian mythology (see her article at www.magdalene.org/pagan_scholars_talk). Also invaluable are the many supportive letters and e-mails I have received over the years from people affirming the value of what I have written. Some have honored me by sharing original artworks or poetry, some have recounted their dreams and visions. I thank them for their confidence in me and for sharing the "journey." My life is made immeasurably richer by the gifts and insights of these fellow pilgrims.

Lilium Regis

O Lily of the King! low lies thy silver wing,
And long has been the hour of thine unqueening;
And thy scent of Paradise on the night-wind spills its sighs,
Nor any take the secrets of its meaning.
O Lily of the King! I speak a heavy thing,
O patience, most sorrowful of daughters!
Lo, the hour is at hand for the troubling of the land,
And red shall be the breaking of the waters.

Sit fast upon thy stalk, when the blast shall with thee talk,
With the mercies of the king for thine awning;
And the just understand that thine hour is at hand,
Thine hour at hand with power in the dawning.
When the nations lie in blood, and their kings a broken
    brood,
Look up, O most sorrowful of daughters!
Lift up thy head and hark what sounds are in the dark,
For His feet are coming to thee on the waters!

O Lily of the King! I shall not see, that sing,
I shall not see the hour of thy queening!
But my song shall see, and wake, like a flower that dawn-
    winds shake,
And sigh with joy the odours of its meaning.
O Lily of the King, remember then the timing
That this dead mouth sang; and thy daughters,
As they dance before His way, sing there on the Day,
What I sang when the Night was on the waters!

FRANCIS THOMPSON

INTRODUCTION

Mary Magdalene: Woman or Archetype?

> For I tell you the truth: many prophets and righteous
> men have longed to see what you see, and they have not
> seen it, and to hear what you hear, and have not heard it.
>
> MATTHEW 13:17

Centuries of desert exile stretch behind her as she crosses the threshold of the third Christian millennium, regal in her bearing, still clasping her alabaster jar. From her new vantage point, she gazes eagerly toward the future with renewed hope. We celebrate her joyful homecoming, embrace her warmly, singing and rejoicing, dancing before her way, as we experience an enormous surge of interest in this woman called the Magdalene, the woman most beloved among the many followers of Jesus Christ mentioned in the sacred texts of Christianity.

The gospels of the Greek Bible assert that a number of women accompanied Jesus during his ministry in the Roman-occupied province of Judea. We have pictured women walking side-by-side with his male disciples, carrying their food satchels and water jars, perhaps trundling carts bearing the belongings of the troupe following the itinerant rabbi Yeshua. And on gospel lists of women closest to Jesus, Mary Magdalene is almost always mentioned first. Apparently she was in some memorable way preeminent—First Lady—in the eyes of the community who knew her.

1

Information like this, read from between the lines of the gospels, encourages us to search the record for the historical Mary Magdalene. As we examine available sources, we sense that her importance is much greater than the biographical details known about her, so scant and inconsistent, though her legends and images have flourished for two millennia in Western culture. The rich tradition of Mary Magdalene's influence and meaning must be examined at levels beyond the literal and historical; she must be encountered on allegorical/symbolic and mythological levels as well. She is not merely a first-century Jewess who was touched by Jesus and knew him well—his ardent disciple, his beloved friend, and first messenger of his resurrection. These details are not disputed. But exalted as these roles are, Mary Magdalene's mythic stature is immeasurably greater: She is the carrier of the powerful archetype of the sacred feminine—the lost bride so long denied in the Christian mythology. In this book we will search for her at these levels of meaning, seeking her many faces, contemplating her example of unconditional love, faithfulness, and compassion, and pondering her union with her beloved bridegroom—bridegroom of Israel and bridegroom of the soul—Christ himself.

Who was this woman whom the four Evangelists called the Magdalene? For more than fourteen hundred years, Christian tradition dubbed her a penitent prostitute, an unsubstantiated and slanderous epithet rescinded by the Magisterium of the Roman Catholic Church in 1969, when it was finally, officially recognized and publicly acknowledged that no scriptural evidence could be found to support the spurious tradition. What do we actually know of this Mary? Why is reclaiming her story of such paramount importance at this moment in our collective spiritual pilgrimage on planet Earth—so important that in some circles it is called the resurrection of Mary Magdalene? Who is this enigmatic woman whose story tugs at our hearts, whose image fires our imaginations, whose song haunts our souls?

Relying on a combination of academic research and intuition gleaned over a period of nearly twenty years, I have become convinced that a missing piece from the foundations of Christianity suggested to my prayer community Emmanuel in 1973 is the sacred feminine embodied in the Mary whom the gospels call the Magdalene—the lost bride of Christian mythology. Her story was distorted and her voice stolen by fathers of the Church who branded her a prostitute, tragically contributing to the dissociation of Christianity from the feminine and thereby unwittingly causing unfathomable suffering in the human family over a period of nearly two millennia.

The momentous repercussions of this design flaw were brought fully home to me on a pilgrimage I made to France in 1996. I stood before the relief carved in the twelfth-century Romanesque tympanum of the Madeleine Basilica at Vézelay, the fourth most popular pilgrimage site in the Middle Ages. As I gazed up at the image of Christ enthroned in celestial majesty above the massive doorway, I realized that his left hand was missing, apparently destroyed in some accident, or perhaps intentionally vandalized. I was stunned. In the preeminent shrine of Mary Magdalene in Western Europe, Christ's left hand—symbol of the feminine and the artistic/intuitive functions of the human brain—was missing! What did it mean? Christ, the heavenly King, enthroned on high and in our Christian consciousness, was maimed—stripped of his feminine partner, ruling from his throne alone. How could he be whole without her?

This loss of the beloved was of inestimable magnitude. Like the pearl of great price hidden in a field—a scriptural metaphor for the reign of God— the tragic loss of the archetypal bride has had far-reaching and damaging consequences for Western civilization and for our entire planet Earth. We pray earnestly for the kingdom to come, but we have—for two millennia— prevented its manifestation among and within us by denying the intrinsic value and importance of fully half that kingdom—the feminine half.

In a homily delivered in the Sistine Chapel on Easter, April 4, 1999, to celebrate the completion of the restoration of its magnificent frescoes, Pope John Paul II quoted from Acts 17:29, ". . . we ought not to imagine that the Divine being is like gold or silver or stone, an image graven by human art and thought."[1] He proceeded, "If the intimate reality of things is always 'beyond' the powers of human perception, how much more so is God in the depths of his unfathomable mystery!" In the same homily addressed to artists, the pope cited Jewish law: "The Law of the Old Testament explicitly forbids representation of the invisible and ineffable God by means of 'graven or molten image' (Deuteronomy 27:15), because God transcends every material representation." Pope John Paul II, speaking in the presence of Michelangelo's famous painting of God creating Adam, thus asserted that this and every other image created by human artists express a false image of God, for God is beyond any human attempt to envision the Divine. Yet Michelangelo's rendering is the prevailing image of God in Western civilization—the Supreme Patriarch, God the Father, honored among Christians worldwide, an image of Divinity made visible, according to doctrine, in Jesus Christ and in his Vicar, the Supreme Pontiff of the Roman Catholic Church.

I have spent the last twenty years and more in search of the lost feminine in Christianity, hoping to restore her to her proper place of honor in our individual minds and hearts, in our consciousness, and in our communal psyche. Some readers may be aware of my earlier books focused on Mary Magdalene as the lost bride. In the wake of the enormously popular mystery-thriller *The Da Vinci Code,* published in 2003, Mary Magdalene's story is being rediscovered and proclaimed all over the world, translated into nearly every language, so that each person can hear the good news in his own tongue—as at Pentecost. In spite of attacks against the credibility of the mystery novel that insist it is merely fiction, Mary Magdalene is exploding into consciousness around the globe as if by spontaneous combustion.

Numerous Christians, predominantly women, gather today in study groups and prayer circles, eager to rediscover and encounter this Mary who was the most faithful of all the disciples of Christ, eager to hear her story and to examine the evidence that speaks of her intimate relationship with the Savior. In finding her, they often find themselves. At last we hear her story, told and retold "in memory of her" (Mark 14:9). She was the abandoned one—exiled, denigrated, stripped of her mantle of honor and dignity by the guardians of the walls. And with her, generations of women suffered similar devaluation and disenfranchisement. Chivalry demands that we seek her out and restore to her the robes of glory that once were hers. Because Mary Magdalene represents an important archetype that embodies a large aspect of our collective human experience, her story resonates with people at many levels, encouraging us to reclaim her now, to call her out of exile, to welcome her home. In remembering and restoring her, we bring home a part of ourselves: acknowledgment of our full humanity, our kinship with one another, our relationship with our living planet Earth and with our environment, our awareness of our own emotions and our own bodies—sacred earthen containers of soul and spirit.

In the years since writing *The Woman with the Alabaster Jar*, I have continued to research Magdalene's story and examine her images in art and lore, gathering information from a variety of sources, rejoicing in their powerful message of freedom and inclusiveness. On my journey I am often asked, "What did we lose when we lost the Mary whom scripture calls the Magdalene?" Simply stated, we lost the color red—the deep crimson of passion, of the blood mysteries, of compassion and Eros in the Jungian sense of *relatedness*. And with the exile of Mary Magdalene from our consciousness, we were tragically cut off from the irrigating waters of intuition and mysticism, from feminine ways of knowing, from the deep wisdom of the body and its senses, and from our intimate kinship with all that lives. These aspects of the sacred feminine were originally embodied in the Mary who was the beloved companion of Jesus and who represented our full humanity in an intimate partnership union with the Divine Logos.

According to Christian scriptures of the Greek New Testament, the historical Mary was a flesh-and-blood person, a close associate of the human Jesus during his ministry, first to encounter the empty tomb and the risen Lord on Easter morning. New light has been shed by various texts found in the Egyptian desert in 1945, the codices of the Nag Hammadi library that speak of her preeminence among the apostles. And research has surfaced showing that the earliest Christian churches were radically egalitarian, allowing women to speak, to teach, and to prophesy in their assemblies. We sense that the model for this elevated status of women among the early Christians was Mary Magdalene, and women worldwide now long to know her better—to celebrate her life, to hear her story, to sing her song. Novelists, playwrights, artists, and songwriters celebrate the return of the bride from her long exile.

We have seen *Jesus Christ, Superstar* and *Godspell;* we have heard Dar Williams sing *The Ballad of Mary Magdalene* and Anne Murray *I Cried a Tear.* We sense her nearness to us and to our own stories.

For decades, women in universities have searched ancient records and mythologies of the Goddess that survive in the far corners of the Earth. *She* is Queen of Heaven, giver of bread, the compassionate, the merciful, the immanent. How ironic it is to discover *Her* at the very heart of Western civilization, embodied in the woman whom Christian tradition vilified as prostitute—effectively silencing her voice for nearly two millennia and, with it, the voices of countless generations of her daughters.

Historical records concerning Mary Magdalene's life are nonexistent: No birth, marriage, or death certificate survives that would prove that this Mary ever existed, nor do we have such documents attesting to the historical Jesus. Even for Jesus, the historical written record is meager: Saint Paul's Epistle to the Romans (A.D. 56–58) contains the first written witness to Jesus, asserting that he is the offspring of King David "as to his human nature." Our gospels are in part a *midrash,* or interpretation of the promises and prophecies made to King David and his heirs about their future dominant role, a theme carried over to the medieval heresy of the Holy Grail. According to the testimony of the authors of all four gospels accepted as canonical, a woman known to the community as Mary the Magdalene walked and spoke with Jesus; she was one of several generous women who supported his ministry with their wealth; she attended the Crucifixion and returned at first light on the third day to the garden tomb, where she encountered Jesus resurrected. Everything else we know of this Mary we must read from between the lines of the texts left to us by the four evangelists and by the authors of the gnostic gospels, dating from the second through fourth centuries.

More than one face of Mary Magdalene emerges from these texts: She was committed disciple, ardent devotee, and intimate companion of Jesus, even his consort or partner, according to various accounts. She is recognized as apostle by some, priestess by others, sometimes beloved and wife. Gnostics equated her with the Sophia, while orthodox believers associated her with the bride in the Song of Songs and medieval troubadours sang of their Dompna—the Lady. We will examine these faces of Magdalene, immersing ourselves in lore and legends gathered over two thousand years by those who sensed her importance to the Christian story and longed for her return to a place of honor—for Mary Magdalene is more than a woman who walked in Palestine, attentive to the words of the Savior and carrying the water jar from which he slaked his thirst.

At the core of her mythology, Mary Magdalene represents the land and the people—Jerusalem, the Daughter of Zion (Sion)—and, by extension, the entire human community, pilgrims on a journey toward union with the Divine. This powerful mythology became incarnate during the first century in the historical person named Jesus, the anointed bridegroom of Israel, who loved his bride (the Church) and "delivered himself up for her" (Ephesians 5:25). In her fidelity and devotion to Christ, Magdalene represents the faithful community who hears his voice and follows his teaching, remaining open and alert to his guidance, ever eager to do his bidding. Hers is the way of the heart, the way of the visionary who eagerly hears and answers the call of the beloved.

Students of Christian scripture find Jesus cast in this role of Eternal Bridegroom in numerous parables and metaphors of the New Testament. How can they fail to notice the woman who, in those cited texts, represents the community, the land, and the people as archetypal bride? How can they ignore the woman identified with the entire community of converts as well as with each individual soul in its ardent seeking of the beloved Divine? Here we will take a new look at these powerful themes and relate them to our own spiritual quest and longing, our own path of enlightenment, conversion, and transformation. The search for Mary Magdalene calls us to examine this story, culminating in the celebration of the wedding feast of the Lamb and the New Jerusalem, the enlightened community arrayed as a bride for her nuptials (Revelation 21:2).

Come, let us examine together the hidden legacy of Mary Magdalene—the greatest story never told!

"The Spirit and the Bride say 'Come!' " (Revelation 22:17).

1

Mary, Mary

They came upon me, the guardians of the walls. They beat me and wounded me and stripped my mantle from me . . .

SONG OF SONGS 5:7

For two millennia, Christian traditions have honored several women from the gospels of the Greek New Testament who bear the same name—Maria. Their shared name in Hebrew is Miriam, or Mariam, derived from the name of King Herod's Jewish queen Mariamne, the last princess of the Maccabean lineage, beloved of her people. The name Mariam was especially popular in the early first century, so popular that the gospels mention five or six women who share the name, which has caused considerable confusion among the identities and roles of the women closest to Jesus.

From earliest childhood, Christian children are told stories of the Virgin Mary, the mother of Jesus, including her acceptance of the message delivered by the angel Gabriel that she would bear the Son of the Most High and call his name Jesus. Children hear about the birth of her special baby boy in the stable at Bethlehem, and about the shepherds and kings who paid homage to him there. As they grow older in the Christian faith, children learn of other Marys mentioned in the gospel stories about Jesus. Of these, the two most prominent are the sister of Martha and Lazarus from Bethany and a woman called the Magdalene

8

who supported the ministry of Jesus from her own personal wealth and was his most ardent and faithful disciple.

While the Mary who is the mother of Jesus has received robes of honor in Western civilization and titles commensurate with the exalted dignity of her role, the Mary who was the beloved companion of Jesus was sadly stripped of her rightful robes of honor and relegated to enforced exile. Symbolically in the ancient Near East, stripping a woman of her mantle or veil dishonored her. It was equivalent to—even a metaphor for—rape. This second Mary was denied her true identity; her story became distorted and her voice silenced by the ugly epithet *prostitute,* and, like her people in Diaspora, she was consigned to the wilderness. In this role, scorned and vilified, she embodies the mythology of both the Greek Sophia and the Jewish Shekinah. In her, Holy Wisdom—who reveals the feminine face of God and is his mirror and his delight—now becomes the abandoned one, the desolate and forsaken bride. She is the bearer of the archetype of feminine consciousness, likewise denigrated and reviled, relegated to second-class status. Like the bride in the Song of Songs, she serves in bondage to the masculine principle. The bride in the Song is black, swarthy from her labor in her brothers' vineyards. Her own, she has not kept (Song of Songs 1:5–6). The woman in the Christian story who in person embodies this principle is the beloved of Christ, the woman called the Magdalene, now reemerging to claim again the robes of her long forgotten glory.

Already in the first century, in the early hours of the Christian story, Mary of Bethany became mingled with Mary Magdalene in the eyes of Christian believers. So inextricably intertwined were their stories that in Western European art, the two are traditionally identified as the same woman. In numerous altarpieces, Mary Magdalene holds the alabaster jar—her identifying icon—in one frame and in an adjacent panel she attends the raising of her brother Lazarus. So ubiquitous was this tradition that in old missals of the Roman Catholic liturgy, the Collect of the Mass for the Magdalene's feast day, celebrated on July 22, contains this short prayer: "We beg, O Lord, to be helped by the patronage of blessed Mary Magdalene, whose prayers obtained from Thee the restoration to life of her brother Lazarus when already four days dead."[1]

Since 1969, however, the Roman Catholic Church has disavowed its long-standing identification of Mary Magdalene with Mary of Bethany and has tried to extricate them from each other, following the tradition of the Eastern Orthodox churches and modern Protestant Bible scholars, thereby repudiating nearly two thousand years of Western lore concerning Mary Magdalene.

The tradition needed to be corrected. Nowhere in scripture does it state that Mary Magdalene was a prostitute. On that point, scholars agree. But I believe this recent revision of the centuries-old tradition identifying Mary Magdalene as Mary of Bethany is a mistake. In an effort to set the record straight on the identification of the preeminent Mary in the Christian gospels, it is important to realize that combining Mary of Bethany with another woman mentioned in an earlier gospel is not the result of a sermon delivered by Pope Saint Gregory I in 591, but rather first occurs in the Gospel of John, probably written between A.D. 90 and 95. The various stories of Mary were braided together early in Christian tradition. The question we must ask is "Why?" The earliest Christians apparently knew of only three Marys: the Virgin, the Magdalene, and the wife of Cleophas.[2] Clearly this was the belief of the Johannine community from which the fourth gospel stems, and is, therefore, indigenous to the canonical New Testament. Perhaps we need to reexamine the evidence for commingling the Marys favored by the earliest exegetes of the Christian story.

Centuries of devout Christians have honored the memory of Mary Magdalene as the repentant sinner saved by Jesus from her sins in a scene from Luke's gospel, believing her to have been the woman who anointed Jesus at a banquet at the house of Simon, though that woman is unnamed in Luke's gospel and in the other synoptic gospels—Mark and Matthew. And yet, John's gospel—written about ten years after Luke's—clearly identifies the woman who anointed Jesus and wiped his feet with her hair. She is Mary, the sister of Lazarus, from the town of Bethany (John 12:3). In this passage, the author of John appears to believe that we already know Luke's version of the story; he is deliberately correcting the account in Luke regarding the identity of the woman who anointed Jesus. John's account also corrects the story with regard to the location of the banquet. Luke places the dinner far away in Galilee, but John, following the earlier and very similar narrative found in the gospels of Mark and Matthew, restores the scene of the banquet to Bethany, situated on the Mount of Olives just east of Jerusalem. This location across the valley from the Holy City has powerful prophetic associations from the Book of Zechariah: "On the Day of the Lord, his feet will stand on the Mount of Olives which will be cleft in two" (Zechariah 14:4). Jesus' anointing at Bethany proclaims his kingship on the prophetic Mount of Olives and must have had immense symbolic associations for Jews eagerly awaiting the coming of a Messiah to save them from the oppression of Roman occupation.

In numerous artistic representations of the anointing scene, Mary kneels distraught, crying over the feet of Jesus, waves of unbound auburn hair streaming over her bare shoulders and down her back (plate 1). This image of Mary Magdalene, promoted in Western art and legend, has served well as a model for passionate devotion to Christ and for the transformation of a sinful life into one deserving of sainthood. Always in the traditional rendering of the gospel story, Jesus is the Savior, Mary the supplicant kneeling at his feet—at the banquet at the house of Simon or at the garden tomb attempting to embrace him after his resurrection. The carnal nature of Mary's alleged sinfulness was thoroughly established in tradition as well, derived solely from the account in Luke's gospel of the anointing by a sinful woman. Because she loved much, much was forgiven her (Luke 7:37–40).

Although the story of the anointing of Jesus by a woman occurs in all four canonical gospels, only Luke calls her a sinner. And yet very early in Christian tradition, Mary Magdalene was conflated, or confused, with Luke's unnamed woman from the streets of Nian; she was assumed to be a prostitute, although on closer examination, the scriptural texts that mention her never supported the slander implied by this tradition.

The Greek word Luke used for "sinner" *(àmartōlos)* is not synonymous with "prostitute" *(porin)*. It has a more general meaning, and would have been used to characterize someone who avoided an obligation or was dishonest in a business transaction. But the sexual connotations of her ill repute flourished nonetheless. Everywhere in medieval art, we encounter the ravishing, sensuous Magdalene, often wrapped in a scarlet or crimson mantle, her sad face framed by waves of deep auburn or strawberry blond hair so often associated with passionate temperament, as in a famous painting by El Greco (plate 2). As the story is repeated over the years, and the portrait painted, gradually her mantle is stripped from her in artistic expression, often leaving a shoulder exposed or, now and again, her bosom. In many Renaissance paintings, Mary Magdalene represents the temptations of the flesh—the sinful, carnal woman in need of forgiveness and redemption. This portrayal is apparently in keeping with the view of Christianity's Church fathers—Saint Augustine outspoken among them—that women, like Eve, who tempted Adam to eat of the forbidden fruit in the Garden of Eden, were a temptation and a distraction drawing men away from their spiritual path.

What does the historical record establish about the woman scripture calls the Magdalene? Like the face that launched a thousand ships, hers sends us forth to reassemble her many images, the extraordinary faces of the one woman who was renowned throughout Christendom as the most beloved and most faithful disciple of Jesus.

Disciple of the Rabbi Yeshua

In addition to reading them collectively as the infallible Word of God, there are other levels on which the scriptures may be read and interpreted as a literary work: the historical, factual or literal level; the allegorical/symbolic level; and the mythological level. Each of these has significant meaning, although they are clearly interrelated as well. Our logical first concern must be to establish the factual, physical or historical record regarding Mary Magdalene. Did she walk side-by-side with Jesus along the narrow streets of Jerusalem and on the garden paths beyond her family's villa in Bethany? Did she stoop now and then to pick a flower at the side of the road or to comfort a child? Did she carry the water jar, pausing along the pathways to offer Jesus a drink?

In our efforts to contemplate the historical life of Mary Magdalene and her close—some sources allege even intimate—relationship with Jesus, we discover only meager evidence. Though exotic rumors abound concerning her origins and family, we have no birth certificate for Mary Magdalene. Primary and earliest of our existing sources are the canonical gospels, written by the four Christian Evangelists—Mark, Matthew, Luke, and John—whose first-century writings were deemed acceptable by the prominent Christian bishop Irenaeus of Lyons (d. 202) and by later bishops following Bishop Irenaeus's recommendations. Faced with numerous versions of the life and teachings of Jesus, some replete with legendary and sometimes wildly speculative material, conservative guardians of orthodox belief made a limited list of sacred texts they considered authentic, declaring other texts of lesser value. In choosing to accept only four gospels, Irenaeus thought he was selecting two texts written by actual eyewitnesses to the life and ministry of Jesus (the apostles Matthew and John) and two others written by disciples of Peter and Paul, respectively—the authors Mark and Luke. Irenaeus apparently believed that these scribes had recorded only information passed on to them by the apostles. He worked relentlessly to discredit other apocryphal and gnostic texts, some of which he deemed blasphemous and others merely of negligible value.

Historically speaking, the earliest written witness to the ministry of Jesus Christ is found in Paul's epistles, recorded several decades after the Crucifixion and attesting to the atoning death and resurrection of the Christ whom the self-proclaimed apostle Paul recognized as the Son of God and Savior. Only after the death of Paul did Christians throughout the Roman Empire become concerned that the story of Jesus' ministry and teachings would be forgotten, and only then were they moved to record their memories of Jesus in written documents. By A.D. 70, the year of the colossal destruction of Jerusalem by Roman legions, Christians realized that the glorious return of Jesus to establish his promised kingdom, as prophesied by Paul, had for some inexplicable reason been delayed. Followers of the Way were now inspired to record stories and sayings of Jesus, relying on material that had survived for a generation in an oral tradition and perhaps in a few early documents, now lost, that may have preserved some actual teachings and sayings of the master, similar to those found in the gnostic Gospel of Thomas.

Of the texts that bear witness to the flesh-and-blood historical Jesus, Mark's gospel was probably written first, in about A.D. 70. Here we find the earliest reference to the woman called the Magdalene who later plays such a prominent role in the life and ministry of Jesus. In the canonical version of Mark, we first encounter this Mary present at the crucifixion of Jesus: "And some women were also there, looking on from a distance. Among them were Mary Magdalene, Mary the mother of James the younger and of Joseph, and Salome" (Mark 15:40). The text goes on to comment that these women had ministered to Jesus in Galilee. Apparently they were among his loyal entourage of itinerant companions who walked with him from village to village in Roman-occupied Palestine. Even this itinerant lifestyle seems unusual in a cultural milieu that had strict traditions concerning the relationship of men and women and their public behavior. We can envision that the women procured food for the group, drew water from the village well, cooked the meals, and washed the laundry, although these activities are not mentioned in the gospels texts.

Mary Magdalene is next mentioned in Mark's gospel when she approaches the garden tomb on Easter. She is one of the *myrrho-phores,* the female ointment bearers who came to mourn the death of Jesus and to anoint his corpse in final preparation for burial. Here, as earlier, she is mentioned first: "And when the Sabbath was past, Mary Magdalene, Mary the mother of James, and Salome bought spices that they might go and anoint him" (Mark 16:1). Because corpses were considered unclean under Jewish law, it fell to the kinswomen of the deceased to prepare the body for burial. The anointing begun on the evening following the Crucifixion had been hurried and perhaps curtailed in observance of the Sabbath law requiring that Jews be in their homes by sundown on Friday. Thus at dawn on Sunday morning, three devoted women returned to the tomb where they had left the deceased body of their beloved Jesus, prepared to finish their ritual anointing of the dead.

The Woman Possessed

While the canonical gospel of Mark mentions Mary Magdalene only at the cross and tomb, Luke's gospel, written later and relying on Mark as one of its primary sources, is more explicit about her role. Luke states that several women whom Jesus had healed of evil spirits and infirmities accompanied him and provided for his ministry from their means. Luke then names three of them: Mary, the so-called Magdalene; Johanna, the wife of Herod's steward, Chuza; and Suzanna. Of Mary, he asserts that she was the one "from whom seven demons had gone out" (Luke 8:2). From this passage, we infer that wealthy women traveled with Jesus and his entourage of male disciples as they made their way through the little fishing and farming villages of Judaea, preaching the glad tidings of the approaching Kingdom of God. Luke's assertion that Mary Magdalene was one "from whom seven demons had gone out" may refer to her having been healed of illness, for people of that time often attributed unexplained diseases to demonic possession. Sources contemporary with the gospels use the metaphor of demonic possession for disease in general, so it is a likely explanation for this passage.[3] Some also suggest the reference indicates specifically mental or emotional disorders, migraine headaches, or possibly severe bouts of depression. We should note that Luke, whose gospel was most likely written between A.D. 80 and 85, is the first of the synoptic gospels to mention demons in connection with Mary Magdalene. Although the final lines of Mark's gospel speak of the seven demons, scholars believe that this passage (Mark 16:9–16) was a late addition to the gospel, probably derived from the allegation in Luke.

Some modern scholars assert that, rather than a historically accurate statement, Luke's allegation of demon possession was an attempt to diminish Mary Magdalene's stature by suggesting that she was unclean and subject to psychological problems of some nature.[4] Perhaps this was a politically motivated attempt to lessen her preeminence, which is inherent in the story of her witness to the resurrection. If Luke was a disciple of Paul, as is widely accepted among New Testament scholars, perhaps he was more interested in promoting the message of Jesus without regard to the importance of the immediate family of the Savior.

Luke's mentor Paul was obviously not popular with Peter or James, the brother of Jesus, acknowledged leaders of the Jerusalem community. Luke may have believed that discrediting or downplaying the family connections of Jesus, as happens surprisingly often in the gospels, would serve the interest of Paul's message and ministry.

Strong political reasons may have motivated gospel writers in the 80s A.D. and thereafter to dissociate Jesus from his Jewish roots and family ties. Their goal was to frame the gospels to appeal to pagan converts from wider reaches of the Roman Empire. They tried to align themselves with Rome, whose legions had just obliterated Israel in a brutal war (A.D. 66–73), culminating in the destruction of Jerusalem and the Temple of Herod and in the fall of the Jewish stronghold at Masada.[5] No proponent of the Christian message would have wanted to be on the wrong side of Rome in this decade; bitterness and rancor between Rome and Israel ran strong at the time the gospels were written, the memory of Nero's duplicitous extermination of the Christians in Rome still burning. In hopes of appealing to converts, the Christian gospels reflect a desire to disentangle faith in the risen Christ from identification with its ethnic Jewish roots and family connections.

Proclaiming the Kingdom of God

A kingdom where justice and loving concern for the well-being of one's neighbor were the prevailing virtues—superseding strict adherence to legalistic dictates of a privileged priesthood—obviously appealed to women who became ardent disciples of Rabbi Yeshua. His proclamation of the Kingdom of God already in their midst was a radical departure from the rules and rituals of Judaism they knew and practiced, and they were charmed by the novel ideas preached by their charismatic master, who often illustrated his points with parables and stories drawn from the daily experiences of women. His teachings included radical assertions about their social status, among them a surprisingly strong position supporting the absolute integrity of monogamous marriage—at a time when divorce was easily obtained by husbands living in a culture that typically viewed wives as items of property rather than people.

Small wonder that women from all walks of life were drawn to this movement, and that those who could left their homes to follow Jesus. They must have been astonished when he cured the woman with the continuous menstrual flux who audaciously reached out to touch his robe as he passed by; she represented the "unclean" status of women in their society. And they must have thrilled at the raising of the daughter of Jairus: Apparently little girls had worth in this new kingdom. Just as surely, they delighted in the story of a widow who swept her house to find a lost coin, rejoicing with her neighbors when it was found; and of another who won the praise of Jesus when she offered alms from her poverty.

These women who followed Jesus must have been elated by the discovery that their charismatic teacher did not maintain the double standard so evident in many of their religion's tenets. When men gathered to stone a woman caught in adultery, Jesus confronted them with their own sinfulness and allowed the woman to go unpunished, exhorting her to sin no more: "Let him among you who is without sin be the first to cast a stone" (John 8:3). Such stories surely touched the hearts of women disciples, among whom the Mary Magdalene was preeminent.

Discipleship

The role of the disciple is to listen attentively to the guidance and wisdom of the spiritual teacher, the master, to ask questions that ensure the teaching is understood as fully as possible, perhaps to walk in companionable silence at times, allowing the teacher to formulate his ideas in solitude, and to support his mission in any way possible—with generous offerings of money, but also with emotional affirmation, enthusiasm, and encouragement.

A narrative found only in the Gospel of Luke records the story of a woman named Mary who is cast in the role of the perfect disciple, a woman who sat at the feet of Jesus, who apparently couldn't take her eyes off him, drinking in every word he spoke, engrossed in his teaching and basking in his presence. At the outset of the community life of the early Christians, Mary Magdalene was identified as this ardent disciple, the sister of Lazarus of Bethany: "[A] woman named Martha welcomed Jesus into her home. She had a sister named Mary, who sat at the Lord's feet and listened to what he was saying" (Luke 10:38–39). In this passage, Martha complains to Jesus that Mary was not helping her to prepare their meal, at which Jesus admonishes Martha, replying, "Mary has chosen the better part and it shall not be taken from her" (Luke 10:42).

I am aware that the nearly-two-thousand-year-old Roman Catholic position regarding the identity of Mary of Bethany with Mary Magdalene was rescinded in 1969 when a revised official calendar of saints' feast days was established. But the entwining of these two female disciples named Mary—Mary called the Magdalene and the one identified as the sister of Martha and Lazarus—is of great antiquity, stretching back to the very dawn of Christian mythology. From the sixth century until the twentieth, no feast day honored Mary the sister of Lazarus in the official Roman Catholic calendar, though one existed for her sister Martha, a feast day that fell exactly one week after Mary Magdalene's own day. Only since 1969 has Mary Magdalene been extricated from centuries-old conflation with Mary of Bethany in liturgical prayers for her feast day. Since then, the liturgy has been stripped of references to raising her brother from the grave.

Important new arguments must be brought to bear concerning the identity of Mary in light of a recently discovered text called the Secret Gospel of Mark.[6] The canonical gospel of Mark accepted by Bishop Irenaeus does not mention Martha or Lazarus and their sister, but a letter written by Clement of Alexandria (d. 215), a prominent Church father and contemporary of Irenaeus, quotes a passage from a text he asserts is a secret but authentic version of Mark's gospel. Clement alleges that certain secret portions of this gospel were reserved exclusively for a special group of initiated Christians because the writings contained material that could easily be misunderstood. In the passage quoted by Clement, we are startled to encounter a reference to the "sister of the youth whom Jesus raised." Could this secret gospel text be the original version of the story of Lazarus's raising found in John's gospel? The obvious answer is "Probably."

The momentous discovery of these passages from a suppressed version of Mark's gospel was made in 1958 by Dr. Morton Smith, an American professor cataloging documents in the monastery of Mar Saba near Jerusalem. The event caused a sensation among Bible scholars when it was published in 1973. Before its discovery, the earliest known reference to the raising of Lazarus occurred in the eleventh chapter of John, written about A.D. 90–95, according to scholarly consensus. Yet here in this recently discovered fragment, we find a reference in an allegedly authentic but suppressed version of Mark possibly written as much as twenty years earlier than John's version of the story and probably antedating the canonical version of Mark.[7] According to Clement, certain passages of Mark were being misinterpreted by gnostic Carpocratians. In the passage Clement quotes from the Secret Gospel of Mark, Jesus and his entourage of itinerant disciples arrive in Bethany and encounter a woman whose brother has recently died. Neither sibling is named. The woman addresses Jesus as Son of David and the disciples of Jesus rebuke her. But Jesus is angry with the disciples and leads the young man's sister into the garden where the tomb of her brother is located. At her request, Jesus raises her brother from the dead. After this, they go to the house of the man and his family in Bethany, "for he was rich."

Which Mary?

If John had access to this suppressed version of Mark when he was writing his own gospel, it might well have been the grounds for merging Mary of Bethany (Luke 10) with the woman who anoints Jesus at the banquet (Luke 7). In John's version, the rich young man from Bethany mentioned in Secret Mark becomes Lazarus, the youth from Bethany of whom Jesus was fond in John 11:3, and whom he raises from death in John 11:43. The story may have circulated in oral tradition, but if so, it is difficult to explain why it receives no treatment in the other synoptic gospels.

The text of Secret Mark continues with a second mention of the sister of the youth from Bethany: "And the sister of the youth whom Jesus loved, and his mother, and Salome were there . . ." This is extremely significant in light of further developments. According to this suppressed text, an unnamed woman identified as the sister of the rich young man from Bethany "whom Jesus loved" traveled with the mother of Jesus and another woman called Salome. This early testimony is clearly significant because the sister of the youth is mentioned *before* the mother of Jesus and Salome, giving her textual preeminence in the group, and the epithet "whom Jesus loved" is later found referring to Lazarus and his siblings in John's gospel where the author elaborates on the story of the young family of siblings in Bethany, stating that Jesus "loved Martha and her sister Mary and Lazarus" (John 11:5). This chapter in John is the only gospel passage in which Jesus is said to love anyone by name, which in itself is significant. And here John states also that this same Mary, the sister of Lazarus, anointed Jesus with her perfumed ointment and wiped his feet with her hair (John 11:2).

These passages concerning the family from Bethany do not occur in the canonical gospel of Mark approved by Irenaeus, but according to his contemporary Bishop Clement, they are part of an original, authentic teaching of Mark. If so, they provide us with critical evidence of a very early conflation of Mary Magdalene with the sister of the rich youth from Bethany—which John's gospel later systematically embellishes. Secret Mark does not name the sister of the rich youth, but at the end of the canonical version of Mark's gospel, we find a further mention of three women traveling together, similar to the group listed earlier in Secret Mark. The testimony of Mark is clear: Three women remained close to Jesus—the Mary known as the Magdalene, his devoted mother Mary, and Salome.

During Jesus' crucifixion, his grieving women followers were gathered nearby, and among the women identified in each gospel account is Mary Magdalene. The mother of James the younger (sometimes called *the less*) and of Joseph (or Joses), also mentioned in Mark and Matthew, is there as well, along with Salome. This is another very intriguing assertion in the earliest version of the gospel, because the texts Mark 6:3 and Matthew 14:7 both name four brothers of Jesus: "James, Joses (or Joseph), Simon, and Jude," stating that he also had sisters, who remain unnamed. These passages have led a number of scripture scholars to suspect that "James the younger" is an abbreviated form of an original phrase, "James the younger brother of Jesus." John's gospel does not mention Simon or Jude, the other two sons mentioned in Mark 6:3, but states succinctly that Mary Magdalene; Mary, the mother of Jesus; and her sister were witnesses to the Crucifixion. Could it be that these women mentioned in John's account are actually the same three women found in Mark 15:40?

The author of the gospel attributed to John has the advantage of the other gospels as sources for his own. In my view, the most obvious way to reconcile these differing accounts is to accept that the three women watchers were the same in each instance: Mary Magdalene; Mary, the mother of Jesus (and of his brothers, including James and Joses/Joseph); and a woman called Mary Salome or Salome, who was either the sister of the Blessed Mother or one of the sisters of Jesus mentioned but not named in Mark 6:3. Due to the conflicting testimony of the gospels, the identity of this third woman remains ambiguous, but the identity of the other two is not.

In the canonical Mark, the same three devoted women followers of Jesus seek his garden tomb at dawn on Easter morning. They are the three myrrhophores, coming to anoint the deceased: Mary Magdalene; Mary, mother of James (Μαρια Ιακωβον); and Salome (Mark 16:1).

Here the woman called the Magdalene is again mentioned first, while her companion is called "Mary, mother of James," referring to her eldest living son, because her firstborn is presumed deceased. A few lines earlier, in Mark 15:47, Mary Magdalene and Mary, "the mother of Joseph," observe the entombment of Jesus. In reconciling the texts of Mark 15:47 and 16:1, a likely deduction is that the companion of Mary Magdalene at the tomb was the mother of both James and Joseph, already identified as the brothers of Jesus himself, rather than the mother of the sons of Zebedee, James and John, as is very often assumed. Indeed, in Matthew 27:56, the Mary present with the Magdalene at the cross is again called the "mother of James and Joseph," and still another woman, the mother of Zebedee's sons, is mentioned with them.

And yet another Mary is mentioned in John's gospel: "Now there were standing by the cross of Jesus his mother and his mother's sister, Mary of Cleophas, and Mary Magdalene" (John 19:25). In reconciling these textual discrepancies, it seems logical to assume that Mary Magdalene and Mary, the mother of Jesus, James, and Joses (Joseph), were together at the cross and at the tomb, accompanied by a third kinswoman, whose identity varies in the three different accounts: Mary of Cleophas (John 19:25) or the mother of the sons of Zebedee (Matthew 27:55) or Salome (Mark 15:40).

In Luke, the women who followed Jesus from Galilee are standing in a cluster, observing his crucifixion from a distance (Luke 23:49). These female companions are not named, but in Luke 8 they are identified as Mary Magdalene, Joanna, and Susanna and many others; and in Luke 24:10, the women at the grave who reported the resurrection to the apostles are named Mary Magdalene, Mary the mother of James, and Joanna. None of the four versions of the passion narrative agrees regarding the women at the cross and tomb. But the one woman consistently mentioned by name in all four accounts is the one called the Magdalene. That in itself is significant.

In the earliest account of Easter morning—Mark 16—the third woman in this group of mourners arriving at first light to visit the tomb in the garden is Salome, the name also mentioned third on the list in Secret Mark, which many scholars after years of debate now concur antedates the canonical version of the text, making it the earliest Christian testimony. Salome reappears later as Mary Salome in legends of Provence, where she is styled as a companion in exile of Mary Magdalene and Mary Jacobi (again, "Mary of James"). An amazing story from the southern coast of France alleges that these three biblical women sought refuge on the shores of Gaul a decade after the Crucifixion, still traveling together as a close-knit group of kinswomen, perhaps reflecting the three archetypal aspects of the feminine in the life of any man—his sister, his wife, and his mother. These roles of the female echo the classical phases of the lunar goddess: maiden, mother (wife/childbearer), and crone. The theme is brought to our attention more forcibly in that the legend names all three women Mary, a name intimately associated with the sacred feminine by the literary convention of *gematria* so prevalent in the gospels.[8]

I think it probable that this identification of the three women as the three Marys in French legend was reflected in the gnostic Gospel of Philip, a text from the late second or early third century that mentions three Marys: "There were three who walked with the Lord: Mary his mother, and his mother's sister, and Miriam Magdalene, known as his companion. For him, Miriam is a sister, a mother, and a wife."[9] This text appears to describe the same three women known to have traveled with Jesus and to have remained faithful to him until his death, the three honored as the "unguent bearers" in Mark's gospel—Mary Magdalene; Mary, "mother of James," and Salome, who was either the aunt or, more probably in my view, the youngest sister of Jesus. The confusion of Marys in the gospels is most easily explained by the hypothesis outlined above. In all likelihood, the authors of the gospels were themselves confused about the identity of the many Marys—or perhaps someone later tampered with the texts, obscuring the identity of these women to preserve an evolving Church doctrine of the perpetual virginity of the mother of Jesus.

Following the Second Vatican Council, as noted earlier, the Roman Catholic Church in 1969 officially rescinded its almost-two-thousand-year tradition that Mary Magdalene was a penitent prostitute, finally acknowledging that no scriptural evidence existed for this slander. Adopting Eastern Orthodox tradition, the Roman Catholic hierarchy now confidently asserts that Mary Magdalene is not Mary, the sister of Lazarus from the town of Bethany just east of Jerusalem. Instead, the Mary called the Magdalene is now firmly declared to be from a village called Magdala on the shores of the Sea of Galilee. This is the standard explanation of her epithet, widely accepted because it has been repeated so many times.

How, then, do we explain why, for the preceding fifteen hundred years, Catholic tradition held that Mary of Bethany and Mary Magdalene were the same person—the ointment bearer, anointer of the Messianic king? In a later chapter, we will examine the older tradition that these two Marys were one and the same, and that the title of Magdalene was not and cannot be a reference to her alleged hometown in Galilee but is rather an honorific given to this intimate companion of Jesus, reflecting her preeminent status among the earliest Christians—those who actually walked with Jesus, sharing his path and promulgating the good news of the Kingdom of God all around them and in their midst.

In discussing the various gospel passages about the women who followed Jesus, we have consolidated testimony about several of the many Marys mentioned, reducing them to three: Mary of Bethany, called the Magdalene by the Christian community; Mary, the mother of Jesus and his siblings; and Mary of Cleophas. Because parents do not commonly call their daughters by the same name, it is unlikely, though not impossible, that the sister of the Blessed Mother was also named Mary. I consider it more likely that a sister of Jesus was called Mary Salome or simply Salome. For our purposes here, we are most concerned with the disciple Mary and the mother Mary, who apparently traveled together and were mutually supportive in their devotion to Jesus and his ministry. Like Naomi and Ruth in that other biblical story of devotion, they provide a model for filial loyalty, a model made visible in medieval Christian art depicting the Crucifixion, deposition, and entombment at which both women attend Jesus.

We have now established that a single woman named Mary, sister of a youth named Lazarus, was a prominent disciple of Jesus. She was apparently his most faithful friend and follower, a close companion of his mother and aunt (or sister), and, with them, loyal to him until the end, when so many of the male disciples had failed him. This is the powerful testimony of the historical record found in the gospels of the Christian scriptures.

Significant questions remain: Was this the full extent of this woman's unique relationship with Jesus? Was she merely a student of an itinerant Jewish rabbi and his most loyal female follower? Or was she, in fact, much more than his most ardent disciple? And if she was from Bethany rather than from a village called Magdala, why was she called the Magdalene?

2
Apostle to the Apostles

Mary Magdalene came and announced to the disciples,
"I have seen the Lord and these things he said to me."

JOHN 20:18

The first rays of dawn had not yet reached the watchtowers of the Holy City. Mary drew her dark woolen mantle closely around her, carefully making her way in the dim light along a narrow path toward the garden tomb where she and her companions had laid the body of Jesus on Friday evening just as the *shofar* sounded, summoning them to observe the Sabbath. In several gospel accounts, Mary came with other women to the tomb, but in John's gospel, the Mary called the Magdalene alone is mentioned, approaching the tomb when it was still dark. How intense was the devotion this woman felt for her teacher, Rabbi Yeshua! The most distinguishing feature of the woman scripture calls the Magdalene is her complete and unswerving devotion to Jesus. This fact is not disputed. The scholarly controversy around Mary Magdalene arises from questions about her actual relationship with Jesus. But, as we established in the last chapter, the New Testament gospels agree on several points: This woman used her wealth to support the ministry of Jesus; according to the testimony of Luke, in a phrase copied later into the final chapter of Mark, she was healed of possession by seven demons; and, according to accounts in all four gospels, she was present at both the crucifixion and entombment of Jesus. What kind of profile can stand on such sparse factual evidence?

Yet, relying solely on the information in the four synoptic gospels, Bible scholars have developed a case that Mary Magdalene was an apostle comparable in status to Peter, James, John, and the rest of the twelve so prominently featured in New Testament accounts. This view of Mary is derived from Eastern Orthodox teaching, which officially honors her as the Apostle to the Apostles, a title suggesting her precedence over the twelve male disciples of Jesus.

But the testimony of the gospels is that Mary carried only one message, albeit an important one, on only one occasion: She announced to the eleven remaining apostles that Jesus was risen, but she was not believed. The precedence inherent in the title Apostle to the Apostles, even though severely limited to one event, was apparently unpalatable to later generations of Roman Catholic fathers, who chose instead to allow rumors of sinfulness to stigmatize her.

A detailed look at the canonical scriptures reveals that none of the twelve male apostles called by Jesus and named in the gospels was present at the Crucifixion on the hill of Golgotha. John's gospel mentions the presence of "the disciple whom Jesus loved," but this elusive person is never named and is never called an apostle in the passages that mention him (or her!). By this, we must infer that this disciple cannot be counted among the original twelve apostles, in spite of time-honored traditions of the Roman Catholic Church that name John the beloved disciple. And with the sole exception of this "beloved disciple," the apostles who followed Jesus are strangely absent from the scene of his execution.

The Faithful One

Magdalene's faithful presence at Golgotha provides us with powerful testimony of her steadfast character in the face of acute danger and distress. But her presence at the garden tomb provides irrefutable grounds for her elevated status as an apostle. In each gospel, she is the unimpeachable witness to the empty tomb of the risen Christ and it is she, accompanied by other women, who carries the news back to the male apostles, informing them that the tombstone has been rolled away and that Jesus has either disappeared or is risen from the dead.

Strong evidence must have supported this uncontested testimony of the gospels. Considering that in their first-century milieu, a Jewish woman could not testify in any court of law, we find it hugely significant that this woman is given unparalleled distinction as the pre-eminent witness to the resurrection of Jesus in the four versions of the story officially accepted as historical, even though Peter did not at first believe her tale and rushed to confirm it for himself (Luke 24:11–12). Clearly, the oral tradition, or *pericope,* surrounding the story of the resurrection must have been unequivocal in its insistence that Mary Magdalene was its first witness. If the authors of the New Testament could have found a way to give a male disciple credit for discovering the empty tomb, they would likely have done so. In fact, the apocryphal Gospel of Peter (c. 70–160) reports that Roman guards stationed at the tomb were the first witnesses to the resurrection, and that when Mary Magdalene and her women friends arrived to lament over the crucified corpse, they encountered a young man in a bright robe sitting in the tomb.[1] But apparently the presence of Mary Magdalene at the tomb was so thoroughly entrenched in stories preserved in an oral tradition proclaiming the *kerygma,* or good news, of the risen Christ that all four evangelists retained it in accounts later declared acceptable by the influential second-century bishop Irenaeus.

Bearer of Good News

The root word for *apostle* in Greek means "messenger," and it is precisely this role of messenger that identifies Mary Magdalene as the Apostle to the Apostles. This is prominently asserted in the next-to-last chapter of John's gospel. Mary is weeping alone in the garden near the tomb on Easter morning when she encounters the risen Christ. At first she mistakes him for the gardener, but upon recognizing him, in her joy at finding him resurrected she spontaneously embraces him. Here Jesus himself gives her the apostolic mission: "Go to my brethren and say to them, that I ascend to my father and your father, to my God and your God" (John 20:17). Mary returns to the others with the first expression of the good news: "I have seen the Lord, and he said these things to me" (John 20:18). Springing from this encounter with Christ in the garden, and from her commission as messenger, the tradition of Mary as an apostle flourished for several centuries before the epithet of penitent prostitute gradually eclipsed her honorable image in the traditions of Western Europe cultivated by Roman Catholicism.

But early in tradition, even though the accounts of all four canonical gospels place Mary Magdalene at the tomb, some Church fathers were unhappy with the idea that a woman was afforded the supreme honor of being the first witness to the resurrection—especially a woman perceived as a sinner by virtue of her early identification with the woman who anointed Jesus in Luke 7:37–39. While some traditions sought to establish Peter as the first person to encounter the risen Christ, others proffered the idea that the Blessed Mother was the first to the tomb, although the canonical texts of the New Testament offer no support for either claim. Based on the evidence of the accepted gospels, the woman called the Magdalene was the first to encounter the empty tomb and the risen Lord and to receive from Jesus a direct commission to share the good news of the resurrection with his brothers. In this role, she is the gospel messenger par excellence.

Equal to Peter

Contemporary scholars have reexamined the literary record and have noted significant points that establish the special character and legacy of Mary Magdalene, particularly regarding the issue of women's power and leadership roles in the early Christian community. Women teachers and deaconesses must have been seen as threatening by various Church fathers who gradually succeeded in eroding the influence of women. But honest students of Christianity's sacred texts are confronted with bluntly stated negative testimony regarding the character of Peter in contrast to that of Mary Magdalene. Although the gospel account relates that Peter received the "keys of the kingdom" (Matthew 16:19), he often misunderstands the teachings and mission of Jesus, and is on one occasion admonished for not recognizing that Jesus faced imminent death.

In contrast, Mary apparently comprehends the teachings fully; she even accepts and prophetically proclaims the Messiah's impending death by her act of anointing him: "She has anointed me in advance for my burial" (Mark 14:8; Matthew 26:12). And in John's gospel, Jesus requests that Mary keep the remainder of the precious ointment she used to anoint him for the day of his burial, thus setting up the scene at the tomb when she goes alone to anoint his body and finds him resurrected. Those seeking the foundation on which the Church built the tradition that Mary of Bethany and Mary Magdalene were the same woman need only look to this passage in John's gospel (12:3–7), which explicitly conflates the sinful woman who anoints Jesus in Luke's gospel, wiping his feet with her hair, with Mary, the sister of Lazarus. Here Mary is instructed to save some of her ointment for the burial anointing at the tomb, a role reserved for Mary Magdalene in all four gospel accounts: "Let her be, that she may keep it for the day of my burial" (John 12:7). Early Christians embraced this association, combining the ointment-bearing Mary into one devoted woman, finding this so clearly implied in the fourth gospel.

After the arrest of Jesus in the Garden of Gethsemane, Peter denies his master three times before the cock crows (Matthew 26:74). The senior apostle, styled as the leader of the fledgling community, fails to show up for the procession of the cross through the streets of Jerusalem, and is again notably absent at the scene of the Crucifixion. By contrast, Mary Magdalene follows Jesus through the streets of Jerusalem (plate 3) and is present at Golgotha, surrounded by other devoted women, including the mother of Jesus and, by various accounts, Johanna and Mary/Salome. Peter and the ten other apostles—one would not expect Judas to be among them—are conspicuous by their absence in each gospel account of the Passion. Two rich and influential friends of Jesus, Joseph of Arimathea and Nicodemus—but not his apostles—help the faithful women take the body of Jesus from the cross. The women anoint the body of Jesus with aloes and spices and wrap him in a linen cloth for burial; the men hurriedly lay him in a new tomb hewn from rock in the garden near the site of the Crucifixion (John 20:40–42). One must presume that the other apostles, like Peter on the night when their rabbi was arrested, were afraid to be recognized as his followers. While the chosen male apostles are in hiding, the female friends and kinswomen of Jesus, led by Mary Magdalene, faithfully support him with their presence throughout his agony, and they return to his tomb to minister to him even in death.

The Beloved Disciple

In addition to the wealthy elders Joseph and Nicodemus, only one man lingered at the cross and tomb, lending support to the devoted women gathered in a pitiful cluster at the foot of the cross. He is the beloved disciple whose head rested against Jesus at the last supper just prior to his arrest (John 13:23). The Roman Catholic Church has maintained for nearly two millennia that this favored disciple was the apostle John, son of Zebedee and brother of James "the greater." This assertion is based solely on the testimony of Irenaeus, the bishop of Lyons, who declared that he was told in his youth that the apostle John had written the fourth gospel. The bishop's apparent agenda was to establish the authenticity of John's gospel.

But there is a second opinion, which seems rather more plausible because it rests on the gospel itself. Historically, a number of groups have believed that the beloved disciple was actually Lazarus, the rich youth whom Jesus raised from the dead. In the gospels, there is only one specific incidence where Jesus is said to love someone and that person is named. A message is brought to Jesus from the two sisters, Martha and Mary, residents of the town of Bethany: "Lord, he whom thou lovest is sick" (John 11:1). The Greek verb *phileis* conveys the idea of fondness found in kinship or friendship. The passage continues, "Now Jesus loved Martha and her sister Mary, and Lazarus" (John 11:5), and the root of the verb used here is *agape*. Stronger than the fondness expressed in the earlier message, *agape* means "compassionate" or "unconditional love." Lazarus is never named among the twelve designated apostles, but in light of this testimony of the gospel, he could be the beloved disciple, who is clearly not one of the twelve. If so, he might also be credited with authoring the last gospel, the one that bears John's name—perhaps in collaboration with a community of which he, along with his sisters, was a leader and mentor.

Another widely circulated speculation ably defended by Ramon K. Jusino, a Roman Catholic scholar, suggests that the true beloved disciple was Mary Magdalene herself and that the pronouns in passages mentioning this disciple were deliberately changed from feminine to masculine intending to obscure this identity.[2] Jusino's well-argued case rests on the premise that the preeminence of a female apostle was intolerable to Church leaders in the first and second centuries.

We will discuss later the fact that Lazarus, Martha, and Mary drop out of the historical record directly after the Crucifixion, in spite of the high-profile roles the youth and his sisters play in the Gospels of Luke and John and, at least by implication although not named, in Secret Mark, the recently discovered version of the suppressed Gospel of Mark discussed in the last chapter. Perceived danger from persecutions by Saul (Paul) may have induced Mary Magdalene's friends and kin to keep her whereabouts secret; this would explain also why she first appears in gospels written after Paul's death, probably in the year 67. By that time, she could be mentioned safely, especially if she was known to be dead herself or in secluded exile. Notably, only the last of the four gospels feels safe enough to openly identify Mary of Bethany as the woman who anoints Jesus, and to identify her with Mary Magdalene by virtue of her role as the anointer of Jesus on Easter morning.

The Preeminent Disciple

All afternoon, Mary Magdalene kept a sorrowful vigil at the foot of the cross on the hill of Golgotha, supported by several other devoted followers of Jesus, including his mother and the beloved disciple (possibly Magdalene's own brother, the youth Lazarus), but not Peter, not James, not Andrew or Levi nor any of the others who had been officially called by Jesus to discipleship. The gospels were not written until after the executions of both Peter and Paul in Rome, possibly associated with brutal persecutions of Christians by the Roman emperor Nero in the mid-60s. Only after the death of Paul do accounts of the earthly ministry of the historical Jesus appear in written form. One might wonder if the gospel narratives were written in part to reaffirm the special status enjoyed by women in the early Christian community, and especially to reassert the preeminence of Mary Magdalene among the Messiah's followers, a position significantly absent in Paul's epistles and Luke's Acts of the Apostles.

Exegetes of the New Testament note with some surprise that Paul never mentions Jesus' ministry, his teachings or travels, and has virtually nothing to say about his life on earth. Instead, Paul's epistles discuss theological interpretations of Jesus' crucifixion and resurrection and his imminent return to establish his kingdom—an apocalyptic view obviously at variance with early statements attributed to Jesus about the nature of the reign of God that is already spread out around us, within us, or in our midst. An apparent disconnect exists between these expressed expectations of the kingdom. And we find evidence of a strong rivalry between Paul and the leaders of the Jerusalem Christian community, Peter and James, who is called the brother of Jesus. Because Paul had relentlessly persecuted Christians before his dramatic conversion on the road to Damascus, we might easily understand why Peter and the family of Jesus would distrust him. This may have been grounds, as well, for sheltering information concerning Mary Magdalene's identity and whereabouts from him, protecting her from the self-proclaimed apostle who did not enjoy their full confidence.

For whatever reason, Paul never mentions Mary Magdalene/Mary of Bethany or her siblings in his epistles, the earliest written testimony to the existence of Christian communities, though he does mention several other women who were active in ministry at the dawn of Church history. These prominent women in the early Church included the deaconess Phoebe, Prisca, and Junia; and in his Epistle to the Romans, Paul greets several other women by name—Mary, Persis, Tryphosa, and Tryphaena—and other sisters in their faith community (Romans 16:6, 12).

That these women receive mention at all establishes the surprising fact of their significance. Numerous archaeological excavations of churches dating from the early Christian era include mosaics and frescoes depicting women in ceremonial vestments indicating their official status within the faith community, leadership roles later denied them by the orthodox tradition of an exclusively male priesthood modeled on Jesus and the twelve male apostles.[3] Apparently, women were highly respected teachers and ministers in their own right and they played an important role in the liturgical life of Christian communities from their inception. Only in later generations were they systematically eclipsed. Tertullian (d. 220) was apparently outraged that gnostic sects were ordaining women as bishops, and other Church leaders asserted their authority to curtail the leadership roles of women. In the epistle known as First Timothy—one of several pastoral epistles now acknowledged as a forgery and not penned by Paul—the author states: "I do not allow a woman to teach or to exercise authority over men; but she is to keep quiet" (1 Timothy 2:12). This was in contrast to the earlier widespread practice among Christians that encouraged women's active participation in the faith community.

Not merely unprecedented for the time, the egalitarian nature of the assemblies of believers that sprang up around the example of Jesus were nothing less than revolutionary. Women followers of Jesus did more than serve the men by cooking meals and drawing water from the village well. They apparently taught, preached, and prophesied in those early decades of the Christian experience, presumably exercising these roles on the authority of Jesus, who called them friends and welcomed their contributions. One can almost see him encouraging women to express their ideas and feelings, quietly listening to their concerns, their hopes, their dreams, and their insights. And most favored of them all was the one called the Magdalene.

The Favorite

The canonical gospels never proclaim outright that Mary Magdalene was his favorite, although this is the position that evolved in the gnostic gospels written between the second and fourth centuries. To establish

Magdalene's preeminence among the apostles, we must read between the lines of the sacred texts bequeathed to us. When we consider the most widely accepted view, that stories about Jesus and his teachings existed in an oral tradition for a generation before being written, and when we realize that the accounts were recorded over a quarter century by four different authors in four widely separate communities—and later edited!—we gain a better appreciation of their powerful and consistent testimony about the unique prominence of one woman. In the canonical gospels, eight short lists name women who attended Jesus at various times during his ministry. Each of these lists mentions three women, and on all but one of the eight, Mary Magdalene is mentioned first. In two places in Matthew's gospel we find the phrase "Mary Magdalene and the other Mary" (Matthew 27:61, 28:1). Only at the foot of the cross in John's gospel is the Blessed Mother mentioned first and Mary Magdalene last on the list. In all other instances, when several women are mentioned together, Mary Magdalene is mentioned first.

Based on that knowledge, if we were asked to select the woman who was most likely first lady in their faith community, whom would we choose? The most plausible candidate for this honorific is the one they called the Magdalene, the woman who, in her passionate and loyal devotion to Jesus, became the model for contemplative nuns throughout Christendom. In her faithfulness and service to Jesus, this woman was the acknowledged representative of the collective community—the *ekklesia* (Church)—in her quest for the kingdom of heaven and union with God. In the earliest dawn of Christianity, men and women stood shoulder to shoulder in their efforts to understand and follow the teachings Jesus had given them, walking in the Spirit, following the Way of the heart, and experiencing the promised reign of God already spread out around them—in their midst. Their Way was one of reconciliation, service, and compassion.

The gospel accounts establish clearly that Magdalene was the most faithful and devoted follower of Jesus, steadfast and loyal all the way to Golgotha, and first to witness his victory over the tomb. For present-day scholars and clergy eager to restore women to a position of power and authority in the established Christian denominations, promoting

Mary Magdalene as an apostle equal in status to Peter, and perhaps even *more* important than Peter by virtue of her steadfast devotion, is a compelling agenda. An interesting stained-glass window graces the Église Saint Martin in Limoux, southern France. Jesus holds a golden key in his hand, one of the keys of the kingdom, and he hands a second key, a silver one, to Mary Magdalene, who holds it over her heart. Peter is not present in this scene. Mary is receiving the legacy and the authority represented by the silver or lunar key, representing feminine ways of perceiving reality and knowing the Divine—the intuitive, emotional way of the heart often accessed through enlightenment received by direct experience, intuition, vision, synchronicity, dream, locution, or altered consciousness—in contrast to the way of obedience, discipline, and indoctrination embodied in Peter. Presumably, the meaning of this artistic portrayal in the window is that the golden or solar/Logos key was given to Peter, while Mary Magdalene became custodian of the other key denoting the hidden or esoteric tradition. This theme, so popular among heirs of the gnostic tradition, is further illustrated by tarot trumps dating from the mid-fifteenth century depicting a female hierophant or high priestess/popess in the tradition of the Magdalene. She, too, often holds the other key.

After fourteen hundred years of seeing her as a penitent prostitute, reclaiming Mary Magdalene as an apostle and message bearer who holds ecclesial authority equal to that of Peter is seen by many Christians, especially female clergy of various denominations, as a giant step forward. And it is.

But does it take us far enough? Was the most elevated role of Mary Magdalene that of a messenger sent on Easter morning to carry the good news, the *kerygma* of the risen Lord, to the friends and brothers of Jesus? Our quest for the true and historical Mary Magdalene continues, urging us to an entirely new level of exploration. Having set aside the idea that the Magdalene was a prostitute or sinful woman from the town of Nain, we must explore another face of Mary, clarifying this controversial question: Was the real Mary Magdalene a messenger with power and prestige equal to that of Peter? Is this effort to reclaim her story merely a quest for authority and influence? Or is her story a higher quest—a quest for union? Could she have been the bride of the archetypal bridegroom of Israel—his sacred partner at the very heart of a powerfully transformative Christian mythology? We can easily acknowledge her role as messenger to the other disciples because it is clearly stated in the gospels. But is that all?

We turn now to examine powerful evidence that the Mary called the Magdalene was the beloved of Christ, the lost bride of the greatest story never told.

3

Bride and Beloved

Set me as a seal on your heart, a seal on your arm,
for love is as strong as death . . .

SONG OF SONGS 8:6–7

Following the calendar of Eastern Orthodox Christians, who honored her unique role of Apostle to the Apostles, the Roman Catholic Church traditionally celebrates the feast of Mary Magdalene on July 22. For the Mass celebrating her special day, Roman Catholic theologians, in their wisdom and honoring their early traditions, chose liturgical readings from the Hebrew Bible's Canticle of Canticles, also known as the Song of Songs or the Song of Solomon. The passages of this erotic poetry speak eloquently of the bride seeking her beloved in the streets and of their mutual joy when she is reunited with him. In Christian theology, Mary Magdalene has borne the archetype of the fervent, redeemed soul seeking reunion with her beloved bridegroom, the Christ. A profound esoteric principle applies here: As above, so below. The marriage covenant of Yahweh with his people is a motif that runs throughout the Hebrew Bible in the books of various prophets, and the metaphor is beautifully expressed in erotic language in the Song of Songs. It manifests in the gospels in the actual union at all levels of experience—physical and emotional as well as spiritual—of Jesus and Mary Magdalene during their short ministry in first-century Palestine. Together, hand in hand in the garden, they embody the time-honored mythology of the Divine in intimate partnership with humanity. The tradition of Mary Magdalene as the bride, representing her land and her people, goes back to the earliest days of Christianity, so we should not be surprised that for so many centuries the Collect of the Roman Catholic Mass on her designated feast day echoed this theme.

The lesson for the Mass quotes the bride: "Set me as a seal on your heart, a seal on your arm," and speaks of the bride seeking her beloved. The Collect also mentions her brother Lazarus. But more astonishing than these was the offertory prayer designated for Mary Magdalene's feast-day liturgy, taken from Psalm 45, the "Nuptial Ode of the Messianic King":

> *The daughters of Kings do thee honor.*
> *At thy right hand stands thy royal bride*
> *dressed in a vesture of gold,*
> *all hung about with embroidery.*[1]

What could have moved the good fathers of the Roman Catholic Church to include these scripture passages in the official liturgy celebrating Magdalene's feast day? Why were they inspired to connect her with the nuptial song found among the Psalms in the Hebrew Bible? For how many centuries were these passages read and reread on her special feast day? How many Western European artists over the centuries painted Mary Magdalene dressed in gold brocade, the robes of the Messiah's royal bride, "whose raiment is threaded with spun gold" (Psalm 45:14). A painting called the *Resurrection of Lazarus,* by Juan de Flandes (d. 1519), shows Mary kneeling at the casket of her brother as he rises from death. She is dressed in gold brocade embroidered with vines, a frequent motif in European portrayals of Mary Magdalene. The vines are a symbol of fertility and also of the royal lineage of the princes of Judah, "God's cherished plant"(Isaiah 5:7).

To cite another painting, Luca Signorelli's magnificent Magdalene (plate 4) arrayed in the embroidered golden vesture of the royal bride carrying her alabaster jar, is a regal image of Mary, the beloved. The

PLATE 1: Peter Paul Rubens (1577–1640), *Supper in the House of the Pharisee.* Hermitage, St. Petersburg. Courtesy of Scala/Art Resource, NY.

PLATE 2: El Greco (1541–1614), *Saint Mary Magdalene in Penitence with the Crucifix*. Museum of Fine Arts (Szepmuveszeti Muzeum), Budapest. Courtesy of SuperStock.

PLATE 3: Peter Paul Rubens
(1577–1640), *Christ with Penitents*.
Alte Pinakothek, Munich. Courtesy
of Kavaler/Art Resource, NY.

PLATE 4: Luca Signorelli
(c. 1441–1523), *Mary Magdalene*.
Museo dell'Opera del Duomo,
Orvieto.

PLATE 5: Jan van Scorel
(1495–1562), *Mary Magdalene*.
Rijksmuseum, Amsterdam.

PLATE 7: Geertgen tot Sint Jans
(c. 1460–c. 1495), *The Resurrection of
Lazarus*. Louvre, Paris. Courtesy of
Erich Lessing/Art Resource, NY.

PLATE 8: Charles Desvergnes
(c.1860–c.1928), Statue of
Mary Magdalene. Basilica of La
Madeleine, Vezelay, Burgundy.
Copyright © Dave G. Houser/
Corbis.

deep crimson of her velvet cloak recalls her flesh-and-blood human nature. On her exposed foot we see the string lacings of her sandal, echoing another line from the Song of Songs: "How beautiful are your feet in sandals" (Song of Songs 7:1). Magdalene's sandal is a mesh of tiny Xs, a favorite symbol of adherents to the medieval Church of Love who honored her as Domina.[2] The letter X shows up in numerous paintings of Mary Magdalene, including paintings by Jan van Scorel (plate 5) and Rogier van der Weyden (plate 6). In the former, Xs are formed by strands of pearls running up the sleeve of her left arm, and the gold brocade rests in her lap. In the latter painting, red Xs are embroidered into the gold brocade of her sleeves in a motif of pomegranates, an ancient symbol for female fecundity.

Conflation of the Gospel Marys

As we have discussed, for nearly two millennia, the Roman Catholic Church identified Mary Magdalene with Mary, the sister of Lazarus of Bethany, though this characterization was not maintained in Eastern Orthodox or Protestant traditions and has recently been abandoned by the Catholic Church as well. Since 1969, designated prayers and scripture readings for the Mass celebrating Mary Magdalene's feast day have been replaced with readings that make no mention of her gold brocade wedding gown or the raising of her brother Lazarus from the dead.

The resulting confusion surrounding the conflated identities of two prominent Marys in the gospels prevents us from knowing how to honor the enigmatic woman whose feet, beautiful in sandals, must have tired as she journeyed with Jesus and his entourage of disciples to coastal villages and outlying hamlets of Galilee and Judaea. In 1969, when the Roman Catholic Church revised its official calendar of saints, the Magisterium responsible for correct teaching also tacitly admitted that Mary Magdalene was not a prostitute, as tradition had maintained for nearly fourteen hundred years of Church history, though they failed to proclaim this enlightened revision from their pulpits. Fortunately, the restoration of her good name has now received widespread acknowledgment in Christian churches and in the media, based on the recognition that no shred of evidence can be found in the gospels indicating the historical woman called the Magdalene was ever a harlot.

In our first chapter, we easily recognized Mary as a disciple, ministering to Jesus from her wealth, because that role is irrefutably asserted in the gospels themselves. But for nearly two millennia in Western art, the Mary called the Magdalene is ubiquitous both in sculpture and in painting, most often identified by the alabaster jar of precious ointment in her hand. She is universally characterized as the ointment bearer, an iconography widespread in European art, based on the association of the woman named Mary who anointed Jesus at the banquet with Mary Magdalene, who approached the tomb in the dawn of Easter morning to complete that anointing.

A modern trend among Bible scholars attempts to separate the two women especially devoted to Christ—Mary of Bethany and Mary Magdalene. First, these scholars mistakenly assert that the tradition of combining the two Marys originated in a sermon delivered by Pope Gregory I in 591 at the Church of Saint Clement in Rome. In his homily, the pope declared that Mary Magdalene was the sinful woman in Luke's gospel and further identified her with Mary of Bethany, the sister of Lazarus who anointed Jesus (John 12:3). Pope Gregory proceeded to discuss her conversion from a life of forbidden acts and sinful pleasures to one of penance, specifically mentioning her unguent and kissing the feet of Jesus.

While this sermon officially sealed the conflation of the anointer of Jesus with Mary Magdalene, Pope Gregory was by no means the first to conflate the two women disciples. He merely stated an association widely accepted from the earliest days of the Church—that the Mary who anointed Jesus at the banquet was the same woman who came to anoint his body at the tomb. Nearly three hundred years before Gregory's sermon, Hippolytus of Rome (170–236) identified the woman called the Magdalene with the sister of Martha and Lazarus. In his commentary on the Song of Songs, Hippolytus also associated Mary of Bethany with the bride from the Canticle, placing Mary and her sister Martha at Jesus' garden tomb on Easter morning when they encountered the risen Lord.

This account of Mary-Martha at the tomb, found in the work of Hippolytus, clearly disagrees with the official version in the canonical gospels, in which the Mary mentioned by name at the sepulcher is invariably Mary Magdalene, and in which no mention is made of her sister, Martha. No canonical gospel places the two sisters of Lazarus at the tomb, so the assertion of Hippolytus that Mary and Martha of Bethany were present there is an anomaly. Apparently Hippolytus assumed the connection implying that the two Marys—Mary Magdalene and Mary, the sister of Lazarus—were really one and the same person, and that her sister, Martha, probably accompanied her on Easter morning. But if so, on what grounds was this assumption made? It is not stated so in the gospels.

As we have noted, the *only* woman mentioned in all four canonical accounts as a witness to the Crucifixion and arriving at dawn on the third day to anoint the Savior's body is the Mary called h Magdalhnh. *The Catholic Encyclopedia* entry for Mary Magdalene, written in 1910, asserts that Mary of Bethany and Magdalene are the same person, citing a passage in John's gospel that makes it nearly impossible to deny.[3] When Judas complained that the sister of Lazarus wasted valuable ointment of nard, lavishing it on the feet of Jesus, the Lord defended her action: "Let her be, that she may keep it for the day of my burial" (John 12:7). How, then, in light of this passage, could Mary of Bethany not be the ointment bearer at the tomb on Easter morning, considering that she had only a few days before received the instruction from Jesus himself to conserve her unguent to complete his burial anointing. Here in John's gospel, the anointing at the banquet and the anointing at the tomb are intimately linked, so we might expect that early Christians associated the two scenes in the gospels, easily identifying the bearer of fragrant ointment as a single person.

In view of her anointing Jesus at the banquet, we would not expect this passionately devoted Mary to be absent from the cross or at the tomb of Jesus. Yet it is the Mary called the Magdalene who stands at the foot of the cross, who assists with the entombment, and who is later the preeminent witness of the resurrection. She is given her title h Magdalhnh in John 19:25, 20:1, and 20:18, but is simply Mary in John 20:11 and 20:16.

The report that Mary was the first witness to the resurrection must have enjoyed enormous credibility among early Christians, because each of the four primary evangelists attests to it. It was obviously so well known to the community that it could not be denied! Like the anointing by the woman with the alabaster jar, the pericope bearing the story of the first witness to the risen Lord was told and retold in memory of her.

Yet surprisingly, in spite of the widespread credibility of these accounts, the third-century commentary of Hippolytus asserts that Mary-Martha came to the tomb seeking to anoint the Lord. From the context, he is obviously referring to the role of Mary Magdalene as told in the gospel narrative, and he identifies *her* search for the beloved with the action of the bride seeking the bridegroom in the Song of Songs. We might assume that it was on the basis of the commentary of Hippolytus that the Roman Catholic Church until very recently read the significant passages from the Song of Songs on Magdalene's feast day—passages recalling the bride searching for her bridegroom and eventually being reunited with him in the orchard of pomegranates. For Hippolytus, the sisters Mary and Martha mentioned in both Luke's and John's gospels apparently represent ekklesia, the faithful community of believers, as bride of Christ; but in the officially accepted Christian scriptures, Mary Magdalene alone is named in this distinguished role. From this commentary of Hippolytus we can establish that the conflation of the gospel Marys was accomplished very early by Christian witnesses, a view most probably gleaned from the familiar role of the ointment bearer referenced in John 12:3 and perpetuated for two millennia in Christian art.

Hippolytus merely stated in writing—and Pope Gregory I only repeated in his sermon—what everyone who read the gospel accounts or heard them preached already knew: that Mary, the sister of Lazarus, was distinguished by a title of honor that expressed her unique status—the Magdalene—Mary the Elevated, Mary the Great.

The Song of Songs

In spite of its explicit erotic passages, rabbis of Judaism retained the Song of Songs in the official canon of the Hebrew Bible because, in their view, the passionate love of the bridegroom and his dark bride, the "fair Shulamite," was an allegory of Yahweh's marriage covenant with his own beloved, the chosen people of Israel. This powerful poetry, full of sensual images and symbolism, was so beloved in first-century Israel that two copies were discovered among the Dead Sea Scrolls, probably hidden in earthen jars in about A.D. 68 during the Jewish rebellion so brutally squelched by Rome's legions. The scrolls were found in Cave 4 near the ruins of the desert compound at Qumran and attest to the popularity of the Song at a time contemporary with the origins of Christianity and the appearance of the earliest gospel. The Song of Songs was so familiar that it was sung in wine houses during the decades that followed, well into the second century. Rabbi Akiba, a prominent second-century Jewish sage and religious leader, apparently thought highly of the sacred wedding song. He is quoted in the Mishnah Yadayim (3:5), composed in the second century A.D.: ". . . the whole world is not worth the day on which the Song of Songs was given to Israel, for all the Scriptures are holy and the Song of Songs is the Holy of Holies."

The Banquet at Bethany

We now return to the gospel anointing scenes, for they form the centerpiece of the emerging story of Mary the beloved. In fact, the gospel narrative seems to focus on establishing Mary Magdalene as the most faithful follower of all.

In the canonical New Testament, we find one story involving a disciple so passionate that the incident was included in all four gospels, a rare distinction indeed. While the three synoptic gospels of Mark, Matthew, and Luke contain many similar stories, most of them are not repeated in John. In fact, stories included in all four officially accepted gospels number only four: the baptism of Jesus by John the Baptist in the river Jordan; the multiplication of loaves and fishes; the crucifixion of Jesus; and, most astonishing, the anointing of Jesus by a woman who lavished an entire pound of precious perfume on him—worth a year's wage!—in her extravagant act of devotion.

In a book reflecting on his years as a bishop in Poland, Pope John

Paul II made a very revealing comment: "The Gospels do not say that Jesus was ever anointed externally like David or Aaron in the Old Testament."[4] In this book, published in 2004, the pope goes on to explain that the anointing of Jesus was a direct anointing by the Holy Spirit for his special mission. Apparently Pope John Paul II failed to notice the anointing of Jesus by the woman with the alabaster jar. Or was he deliberately ignoring the gospel testimony because it was a woman, not a priest, who anointed the Messiah? Did the pope never wonder at this act? By her action, the woman, who embodied the spirit of the people, proclaimed both the kingship of Jesus and his impending death as the bridegroom/king, the Messiah of Israel.

Considering that women in the time of Jesus were held to be the property of their husbands or fathers, valued on a par with the cow in the shed or the couch in the living quarters, including this story of the anointing by a woman is nothing less than remarkable. Indeed, the memory of this event was apparently so powerful that it survived in the oral tradition for forty years before being recorded by the author of Mark's gospel and later being included by each of the other evangelists intent on recounting details from the life, ministry, and teachings of Jesus. Considering the low esteem in which women of the time were held, it seems especially odd that this particular story received such prominence in the original Christian communities. Who was this woman and what was the meaning of her extraordinary action in anointing Jesus? We need to examine this in light of a first-century Jewish society that embraced strict taboos against a woman touching a man in public. While the apostles complain about her, Jesus himself does not repudiate her or the extravagant act of anointing, affirming instead that she has done him a favor: "She has anointed me in advance for my burial, and wherever this story is told, it will be told in memory of her" (Mark 14:9).

Where else in the gospels is attention drawn to any action as in this case with the admonition to tell and retell the story? Given that *messiah* means "anointed," we are witnesses here to a ritual proclamation of kingship enacted by a woman. In proclaiming the kingship of Jesus and his role as Messiah, this woman has also prophesied his imminent death. And yet how many Christians remember the incident? How many can recall her name? Even Pope John Paul II failed to remember her anointing of Jesus and its enormous significance, dismissing her in a single statement.

The earliest record of the unnamed woman with the alabaster jar of ointment is in the Gospel of Mark. The scene takes place during Jesus' final trip to Jerusalem, just before the Jewish feast of Passover: "While he was at Bethany in the house of Simon the leper, and was reclining at table, there came a woman with an alabaster jar of ointment, genuine nard of great value; and breaking the alabaster jar, she poured it on his head" (Mark 14:3). According to this narrative, the disciples gathered at the banquet were aghast at her action and complained to one another about the value of the wasted ointment, but Jesus admonished them, insisting that the woman had done him a favor to be told "in memory of her" (Mark 14:9).

Apparently the story of the anointing was taken to the heart of the Christian community, because the other evangelists include it, though with some variations and embellishments. While a number of scripture exegetes who interpret the gospel texts literally insist that Jesus was anointed by a woman at three different times (as reported in Mark, Matthew, Luke, and John), this view is, in my opinion, impossible to sustain given the similarities in the texts. Matthew, writing in about A.D. 80, copies Mark's already published version of the anointing nearly verbatim. Then Luke, possibly for political reasons suggested in an earlier chapter, moves the story out of Bethany during the week of Passover—and very deliberately places it much earlier in Jesus' ministry and far from Jerusalem in an obscure town in Galilee (Luke 7:37–50). The story is embellished so thoroughly in Luke's version that it is almost beyond recognition, providing grounds for scholars to claim this was a different anointing by a different woman.

But to support their theory, one must believe that this extraordinary event, a woman with an alabaster jar of expensive perfume anointing Jesus at a banquet, actually occurred on at least two separate occasions. As we will see, the author of the fourth gospel explicitly denies that possibility by combining details from both earlier accounts. The significant elements of the original story in Mark, retained by Luke, are the woman, the alabaster jar, and Simon, the given name of the host of the banquet, although in Luke's version he is no longer a leper but rather a Pharisee. Only Luke characterizes the anonymous woman as "a sinner from the town," and although *àmartōlos,* the Greek word he uses for "sinner," is not the word for prostitute, this sinfulness is the point of Luke's narrative, which recasts the previously anonymous woman with the alabaster jar by bequeathing to her a bad reputation.

The woman in Luke 7:37–38, still unnamed but now penitent, stands behind Jesus and bathes his feet with her tears, kissing his feet and wiping them with her hair while anointing them with her precious unguent. This is clearly the most erotic scenario in the New Testament, and Simon the Pharisee is frankly horrified that Jesus allows this wanton behavior, outrageous—even scandalous—at a time when no Jewish woman would dare to touch a Jewish man in public. Luke's story proceeds to explain that Jesus forgives the woman's sins, declaring that much is forgiven her "because she has loved much" (Luke 7:47). What in Mark's and Matthew's versions was an apparent outpouring of passionate devotion becomes a lesson in repentance and forgiveness in Luke's revision of the story. And still, like so many other women in the New Testament, the woman remains anonymous, even though Jesus himself stated that wherever the gospel was preached, her story would be told, "in memory of her." How could the gospel authors fail to record her name? Perhaps they had an important reason for withholding it.

The Fourth Gospel Anointing

Literalist Bible scholars insist that the anointing event in Bethany is not the same event that occurred in Nain on grounds that the Bible is the unerring word of God and cannot contain contradictions. We might accept their view that the events occurred at two different banquets held at two different cities on two separate occasions if the author of John's gospel had not set about with acute deliberation to correct the record offered in Luke 7, for a very similar anointing story occurs in John 12. Here, as in the earlier accounts, Jesus is reclining, Roman style, at a banquet. But John has returned the story to the village of Bethany and to the period just six days prior to the Jewish Passover festival. And now, for the first time, a gospel names the woman with the jar of precious ointment. In John's account, she is not an unnamed sinner from the town of Nain, as Luke's gospel stated; she is instead well known to us all! She is Mary, the sister of Lazarus, who is also present at the table, and of Martha, who is serving the dinner. Like the early Christians who heard the gospels preached, we are familiar with this family of siblings whom Jesus loved. We are not surprised to find him in their midst.

In passages just prior to this banquet, John related the amazing story of the raising of Lazarus (John 11). At that time, Mary threw herself weeping at Jesus' feet, and he was moved by her tears to raise her brother from the grave (see plate 7). Once again, in John 12, this same Mary weeps at the feet of Jesus, anointing them extravagantly with fragrant ointment and wiping them with her hair. The author of John's version seems to be combining the stories found in the other published accounts into his own narrative, weaving together explicit details from each. Among the synoptic authors, only Luke mentions the woman's anointing the feet of Jesus with her tears and using her hair to dry them (plate 1). But in John's version, an unnamed sinner is not the one who performs this intimate act. Here, as if to correct a misconception spawned by Luke's narrative, the woman is deliberately named: She is the sister of Lazarus. Moved by her earlier tears, he raised her brother from the dead (John 11:43), and now the fragrance of her perfume of precious nard, poured lavishly upon his feet, fills the house (John 12:3).

This fragrance of nard stirs a poignant memory, recalling a scene of which it is an unmistakable echo. In another passage in Judeo-Christian scripture we encounter the fragrance of nard surrounding a king at a banquet; it is the fragrance of the bride in the Song of Songs: "While the king was at his table, my nard spread its fragrance around him" (Song of Songs 1:12). The scenario in John's gospel explicitly calls to mind that detail from the Hebrew Song of the Bride and Bridegroom. The gospel account in John invites us to recall the beloved Canticle.

And the act of anointing itself proclaimed the kingship of the Messiah, prefiguring his marriage. A refrain is found again in the Song of Songs: "How sweet is your love, my sister, my spouse. How much better . . . is the fragrance of your oils than any spice!" (Song of Songs 4:10).

Why was the story of the anointing of Jesus by a woman so important to the early Christians that all four evangelists retained it? Did they consider it merely a spontaneous act of devotion by a passionate woman toward the master? Or might it have been an act of highly charged symbolic significance to early Christians who recognized the action in the historic and religious context of their milieu? Was the anointing of Jesus an isolated event—or an archetypal one?

As we have seen, in his commentary on the Song of Songs, Hippolytus of Rome recognized the bride in the gospels by her presence in the garden, seeking the tomb of the beloved. But he could as easily have recognized her at the anointing during the banquet in Bethany, which may be the reason he explicitly names Mary of Bethany at the tomb on Easter morning. Among ancient pagan rites celebrating the sacrificed bridegroom/king, anointing of the king had sexual connotations. It was the prerogative of the bride, representing the people of her domain, to unite with the king in a marriage ceremony that proclaimed his role as the anointed one—the chosen Messiah. Male prophets and priests later usurped the role of anointing kings of Israel, but more anciently the rite of anointing was associated with *hieros gamos,* the sacred marriage, and was the exclusive prerogative of the royal bride.

The gospel narratives of Jesus' Passion, death, and resurrection, beginning with anointing at the banquet and culminating with the joyful reunion of the beloveds in the garden after the resurrection, provide a virtual reenactment of ancient spring rites celebrated yearly, indigenous to Roman-occupied lands of the Mediterranean basin and beyond. Citizens of the Roman Empire were well acquainted with the pagan liturgies, which were not banned until the end of the fourth century A.D. and apparently survived in remote rural areas well into the sixth century. In assessing this connection between Christianity's sacred texts and ancient pagan liturgies, we must remember that the gospels were written not in Hebrew for a Jewish audience, but in Greek for pagan converts to the Christian Way. Surely they would have recognized the ancient mythology embodied in the anointed sacred king and his faithful bride.

In his commentary on the Song of Songs, Hippolytus reflects this obvious recognition of Mary of Bethany as the bride. Anyone at that time and place could have identified the woman who anointed the king and met him later, after a liturgical pause of several days, resurrected in the garden. After performing a ceremonial nuptial rite proclaiming his kingship, the royal bride enjoyed the prerogative to unite in the bridal chamber with her consort. The nuptial anointing ceremony itself bore obvious symbolic associations with anointing of the masculine by feminine secretions during the joyful consummation of the marriage in the secluded bridal chamber.

For millennia, anointing carried associations with sexual union in poetry of the ancient Near East.[5] Already in the Babylonian epic *Gilgamesh* (c. 2700–2500 B.C.), we encounter this connection of sex with anointing when the hero Gilgamesh tells his friend Enkidu that the prostitute who anointed him now laments his death. In later poetry, the anointing became identified with the nuptial ceremony of the hieros gamos—the sacred marriage uniting the royal priestess representing the Goddess, her land, and her people, with the consort of her choice, the strong man capable of defending her and her domain against their enemies. For millennia, such ritual celebrations had occurred throughout the region, declaring the kingship of the sacred bridegroom. The Messiah was, by definition, the one who was united by marriage to the royal bride.

The word appears to be a phonetic cognate of *messehah,* a phallic pillar associated with goddess worship of Asherah by Canaanites in ancient Israel.[6] Pouring libations over phallic pillars is widespread in ancient pagan rites of the ancient Middle East and India. We have only one story of Jesus being anointed and that, by a woman, is reminiscent of ancient rites of sacred marriage celebrated in honor of other divine partners in the Mediterranean region: Dumuzi/Inanna, Tammuz/Ishtar, Osiris/Isis, Adonis/Venus, Ba'al/Astarte, and other virile gods and love goddesses of Israel's pagan neighbors since time beyond memory. The powerful anointing scenario in the gospels, echoing the liturgical elements of the Song of Songs and other hieros gamos mythologies, seems tantamount to a visual proclamation that Jesus came to embrace the feminine and to reinstate the ancient model for partnership—itself the model for life!—at the heart of the Christian story. The earliest exegetes of Christian gospels, like Hippolytus and Origen, appear to have recognized this connection, but it was later denounced, derided, and eventually suppressed by those unwilling to share power and influence with women in the early Church.

Paul's Testimony

Inadvertently, we have come upon a new and surprising context for Paul's casual comment in his first letter to the community at Corinth: "Do we not have the right to travel around with a *sister wife* as do the other apostles and brothers of Jesus and Cephas?" (1 Corinthians 9:5). Because Paul bears the earliest written witness to actual practices of the first generation of Christians, his words should be taken seriously. What was that he wrote? Did he assert that the apostles and brothers of Jesus were traveling with their sister-wives? What does he mean? Some Bibles have translated the Greek phrase αδελφην γυναικα as "Christian sisters" or "believing sisters." But in Greek, *gyne* means either woman or wife. Thus, these women with whom the men are traveling are either their sister-women or their sister-wives. Because Jewish law frowned heavily on promiscuity while insisting on marriage as an obligation, we should consider giving these couples the benefit of the doubt: They were in all probability married—the prototypical missionary couples!

Another text in the scriptures familiar to Christian scripture authors mentions sister and spouse in the same sentence. The bridegroom in the Hebrew Song of Songs also speaks of a sister-wife: "You are a garden enclosed, my sister, my spouse, an enclosed garden, a fountain sealed" (Song of Songs 4:12) and "I have come to my garden, my sister, my spouse" (5:1). Parallel lines occur in liturgical chants honoring the Egyptian deities Isis and Osiris: "Come to the one who loves you. Come to your sister, come to your spouse."[7] I suggest that the ecstatic poetry celebrating the sacred union in the Song of Songs, known to have been extremely popular at the time of Jesus and his Mary, was a model for the community life of early Christians who traveled as missionary couples from town to town throughout Judaea and the lands of the Mediterranean basin. As we noted earlier, copies of the Song of Songs found among the Dead Sea Scrolls in the caves near Qumran attest to the high esteem in which it was held even in that intensely ascetic Jewish community.

In Luke 10, Jesus appointed seventy-two disciples and sent them out two-by-two into every town; can it be that these were not pairs of men, but actually married couples? The gospel does not say this missionary work was confined to men, but two thousand years of patriarchal overlay has obscured Paul's testimony that early Christian leaders traveled with their wives. Further reading of Paul's letter leads us to conclude that Paul did not provide the model for these couples traveling together. I consider it far more likely that Jesus was the model, traveling with a woman whom we might characterize as his own beloved sister-spouse, echoing verses from the Song of Songs.

When Paul speaks in his epistles about the imminent return of Christ and the coming of the kingdom, he states his opinion that people no longer need to fulfill the commandment to marry. Given that Jewish law demanded marriage of all males, Paul goes against the teaching of the Torah, but apparently he is convinced that time is so short before Christ's return in glory that the law can be waived. Still, as an example for the new lifestyle of celibacy he encourages, Paul doesn't say "Look at Christ" as his model. Instead he says, "Look at me" (1 Corinthians 7:7–8). Can we infer that if Paul had known Jesus to be unmarried, he would have used Jesus as the preeminent example for celibacy rather than himself? I believe so.

These points suggest that the earliest Christians recognized the woman who anointed Jesus at the banquet in Bethany, who met him resurrected on Easter morning, as the bride of their archetypal bridegroom. Together, the pair embodied the powerful, familiar mythology of the sacrificed king and his beloved, a mythology that immediately resonated in every corner of the Hellenized Roman Empire. Because the canonical gospels were written in Greek to encourage Greek-speaking converts in the far reaches of the empire, the story of the anointing, torture, death, and resurrection of the historical Jesus, hereditary king of royal Judaic lineage, likely captured the minds and hearts of those already familiar with the mythology of the sacred union of the archetypal beloveds—the Divine imaged as loving partners. Although pagan rites were sometimes celebrated with orgies, the deeper meaning of sacred marriage rites was understood as an ecstatic celebration of the life force, the generous abundance of the earth, and the cycles of life, death, and rebirth that are the shared experience of the human family. Joy from the ritual bridal chamber spread out into the crops, herds, and families of the domain—and everyone lived happily ever after. The mythic story was not merely about a sexual union, but involved the harmonious dance and symbiotic partnership of cosmic energies manifesting as masculine and feminine as well.

Magdalene—Hometown or Title?

Especially relevant to the controversy discussed earlier—whether two of Jesus' disciples were named Mary or only one—is the meaning of the title the Magdalene. Many New Testament scholars maintain that the Greek title h Magdalhnh probably indicates that the woman was from a town called Magdala.[8] Though no other woman in the gospels has her hometown linked to her name in this way, in this case, this has become the scholarly consensus. Most of the other women in the gospels identified by name are given a title describing them as the mother, wife, or sister of a man. Only Mary the Magdalene has a distinctive title. Bible scholars, seemingly unable to think of any other rationale for her unusual epithet, accept the standard interpretation that apparently stems from the fourth century when Saint Helena, the mother of Constantine, traveled to the town of Mejdol in Galilee and "discovered" the house of Mary Magdalene. Scripture scholars consider rendering h Magdalhnh as "of Magdala" the simplest way to explain the term. Because Magdala was a town in Galilee, the reasoning goes, this woman could not be "of Magdala" and also from the town of Bethany, located on the Mount of Olives a few miles east of Jerusalem.

On this basis, numerous modern scholars separate Mary Magdalene from Mary of Bethany, insisting that they are *not* the same person; in fact, a number of scholars assert that combining the two Marys was an error that began in the fourth century.[9] Numerous modern translations of the New Testament now render Maria h Magdalhnh as "Mary of Magdala." Scholars and translators are apparently adopting this simple or standard explanation for her title, believing it correct without questioning it any further.

I have researched this question for years and have concluded that just because something is repeated numerous times over a period of centuries does not mean it is true. This seems to be the case with the town currently called Migdol (Magdala) located on the western shore of the Sea of Galilee and hailed by tour guides as the birthplace of the Magdalene. I have seen no contemporaneous written evidence that the town of Magdala existed by that name in the first century of the current era. In fact, records from that time mention a different name for the town located on the site where a village called Migdol now stands.

Under close scrutiny, the fact emerges that the town now known as Migdol, situated on the Sea of Galilee just north of Tiberias and accepted as Mary Magdalene's hometown, was known by an entirely different name in the first century A.D., a name that had nothing to do with a tower. According to Flavius Josephus, the first-century Jewish author of *The Jewish War*, describing the Jewish revolt against the Romans (A.D. 66–73), the town now called Migdol (Hebrew for "tower") was known in his day as Taricheae. In the introduction to his book, Josephus states that he wrote the original draft about the Jewish revolt in the early 70s in Aramaic, his supposed intent being to persuade the "northern barbarians" (Syrians and Babylonians) not to revolt against Rome. Writing in Aramaic, his native tongue, for speakers of Aramaic, we might expect Josephus to use the Aramaic name for the town, had there been one. Instead, he uses the Greek name Taricheae without mentioning Magdala.

The prosperous Greek city of Taricheae, which had forty thousand inhabitants, 230 fishing boats, and extensive orchards in Josephus's day, was located on a site apparently once occupied by a fishing village called Magdala Nunayah in Aramaic, a name that meant "tower of the fishermen" or possibly "tower of the fish." The site may have had a fortress at some very early date. The town was located on the Lake of Gennesareth (the Sea of Galilee or Sea of Tiberias), and it had an important fish-processing industry, reflected also in its Greek name designating it a place for processing salted fish. The question is: Was the town called Magdala during biblical times? Evidence shows that it was called Taricheae in Roman records dating from as early as 43 B.C. On March 7 of that year, writing from the camp of Taricheae, *in castris Taricheis,* Cassius sent a letter to Cicero describing a recent battle fought in the region.[10] Almost a hundred years later, official Roman records from A.D. 53 again mention the town, stating that territories including Taricheae and a number of neighboring cities were ceded by Rome to the Jewish king Agrippa II. From the nearly-one-hundred-year span of these dates, we may establish that Romans in occupied Galilee called the city by its Greek name for nearly a century and for at least two decades after the crucifixion of Jesus.[11] In the decade before the city was destroyed by the Romans and its residents slaughtered, the city sported a hippodrome where the Hellenized populace enjoyed horse and chariot races. Flavius Josephus visited Taricheae on several occasions and was present at its capture. He records the destruction of Taricheae by the Roman general Titus Vespasian in A.D. 67, but makes no mention of the town's Aramaic name, if it had one, in any of his writings.[12]

This passage from Josephus becomes important in our quest for the meaning of Mary Magdalene's epithet. The title of the tenth chapter in Book III of *The Jewish War* names both the city Taricheae and the country Gennesareth. In the opening lines of the chapter, Josephus mentions that people of the country call the lake Gennesareth (its Aramaic name). Because he wrote his original draft in Aramaic, this seems logical enough. But logic says also that he might have stated here that the local people call Taricheae by the name Magdala, if that were the case. He does not. He calls the city by its Greek name and the lake by its Aramaic name, which, as we know from John's gospel, the Romans called the Sea of Tiberias (John 21:1). Josephus, writing in about A.D. 70, gives no hint that the Hellenized Galilean city was called Magdala.

I am convinced that his Aramaic audience, as well as the Roman, called the town by its Greek name, which had been in use for more than a century and probably much longer.

As additional evidence, the contemporary first-century *Geography of Palestine,* by Strabo (Book 16:2, 45), mentions that Taricheae is noted for salted fish, and here again, the alleged Aramaic name of the town (Magdala) is not mentioned.[13] Strabo lived from 46 B.C. to A.D. 20, a span that would have included a likely birth date for Mary Magdalene, but the town claimed to be the source of her epithet and where she is believed to have lived was called Taricheae at the time. Pliny (*Natural History,* V, 71) and Suetonius *(Life of Two Caesars)* also mention Taricheae in writing, as do several later sources.[14] The available evidence from biblical times asserts that people traveling, visiting, living, and campaigning in Palestine for a period of almost two hundred years called the town Taricheae.

Conflicting Testimony

Calculating by the distances mentioned in several sources discussed above, we can establish that Taricheae was located on the site now called Migdol, assumed by current scholarship to be the hometown of Mary Magdalene. But the earliest evidence to support the name Magdala for this town on the shores of the Sea of Galilee is in the Jewish Talmud. Composed in the fourth century by Jews relying on oral traditions, this compilation mentions Aramaic names for the town. But considerable confusion exists among various texts of the Talmud about the correct location and identity of the town; several names are given and apparently two or possibly three towns were discussed whose names are related to Migdol. These are Mejdel, Magdal-Geder, Migdol Nunayah, and Magdala Sebayah (or Migdol Sebayah). If there were two or three Galilean towns called Magdala with variations, it appears even less likely that the epithet Magdalene was coined to reflect a town of origin, because it would only give rise to the question "Which one?"

The Talmud Ta'anit says that Magdala was wealthy and immoral, destroyed for prostitution (Ta'anit 4:69c).[15] The allegation of prostitution found in the Talmud may have been symbolic rather than literal, for the town Taricheae was long characterized as Hellenized, meaning that it had adopted the Greek lifestyle and Greek mores. In Hebrew prophecy, chasing after foreign gods and worshipping idols were often characterized as prostitution.

How interesting that later Christians would decide that *this very town,* destroyed for immorality, indeed, for prostitution, must be the birthplace of the Magdalene. Perhaps it seemed to fit so well with the sullied reputation of the sinful woman who anointed Jesus in Luke 7 and a few lines later, in Luke 8:2, was called Magdalene, the one who was healed of seven demons. The conflation of the town of ill repute, the anointing woman forgiven for her sins, and the Magdalene began here—perhaps even before John's gospel was written, because the author of the fourth gospel so clearly attempts to correct the record by identifying the anointer of Jesus as the sister of Lazarus—a woman from Bethany, not Galilee.

A further confusion in the fourth-century Babylonian Talmud Gemara is a reference to the mother of Jesus as *m'gaddela nashaya,* the "dresser of women's hair." The author of this statement seems to be confusing the mother of Jesus with Magdalene on the basis of the latter's epithet, but he makes no reference to the town of Magdala, instead translating "dresser of women's hair" as a euphemism for a loose woman. Apparently that the epithet Magdalene was derived from the name of a town was not an established fact in his day.

Further confusion about the origin of the title Magdalene derives from contradictions in early manuscripts of the gospels themselves. The textual criticism revolves around a passage in relatively late Greek copies of Matthew's gospel that mentions a region called Magdala (Matthew 15:39). This remains a disputed text in Christian scripture; several of the earliest manuscripts (Codex Sinaiticus and Codex Vaticanus, both from the mid-fourth century) have Magaden rather than Magdala in this verse at the end of Matthew 15. The earliest Greek manuscripts of the gospels mention a region on the western shore of the Sea of Galilee called Dalmanutha, in Mark 8:10, replaced by Magadan (or Magedan) in a similar passage in Matthew 15:39.

Odd that Matthew changed the name found in Mark's similar account of Jesus' journey by boat after the multiplication of loaves and fishes. Archaeologists are at a loss to pinpoint either Magadan or Dalmanutha mentioned in these texts.

Piecing together evidence from the fourth- to fifth-century Talmud, we see that the town reverted to an Aramaic name, Magdala Nunayah, after Taricheae was defeated and its citizens slaughtered in A.D. 67. The substitution of Magdala for Magadan in Matthew 15:39 may have been influenced by the Gamara of the Babylonian Talmud, which mentions the Aramaic town Magdal Nunuyah. This suspected corruption of Magadan to Magdala, which probably occurred in about the fourth century, was extended to subsequent Greek copies of the text and, later, their translations into Latin and other languages. Most notably, the translations of Erasmus, Martin Luther, and the King James Bible contain the corrupted spelling, stating that Jesus went in a boat to the borders of Magdala.

The corrupted version of Matthew was widely dispersed in vernacular translations of reformers who followed the text of a Greek manuscript called the *Textus Receptus* (Received Text), published in 1516 and in use by the Greek Orthodox Church. Older manuscripts used by the Roman Catholic Church were not consulted for this translation, so their reading of Magadan (or Magedan) was ignored in the *Textus Receptus* and its numerous derivative translations. The alteration from Magadan to Magdala survives in other Bibles of the Reformation, while Roman Catholic translations have continued to use Magadan (or Magedan), the name given the region in the most ancient, and most reliable, manuscripts of Matthew's gospel. Possibly a Greek-speaking copyist was confused by Magadan, a town he never heard mentioned, and he either consciously or unconsciously rendered it Magdala— whether influenced by Mary Magdalene's honorific, or by the Jewish Talmud, or perhaps by his own knowledge of the geography of Galilee, we will never know. In effect, he created a biblical reference to Magdala that in all likelihood did not exist in the original Gospel of Matthew or anywhere else in the New Testament. In *The Five Gospels,* a translation of the canonical gospels and the Gospel of Thomas, the seventy-four scholars of the Jesus Seminar, chaired by Robert W. Funk, chose to use Magadan in Matthew 15:39. One presumes that the textual evidence they encountered supported that reading rather than Magdala. In that case, the majority of the text's translators must have felt that Magdala was an erroneous reading of the original text of Matthew 15:39.

Taricheae Renamed after A.D. 70

Why does this matter? Must we care if Magadan was changed to Magdala by a well-meaning copyist? Yes. It matters because the strongest reason for the simple and standard interpretation widely parroted, that Mary Magdalene was from a town called Magdala, appears to derive from a belief that the town existed, that it is mentioned in scripture, and that Jesus visited there. If the town of Magdala did not exist by that name in Jesus' time, if he never visited it, and if it was only later called Magdala, then we may begin to suspect that the town in Galilee received its name from Christians attempting to determine the birthplace of Mary whose title was the Magdalene, not the other way around. I believe the name was given to the new town raised over the ruins of Taricheae in an *ex post facto* attempt to explain the enigmatic title of this woman. Zealous Christians eager to discover the meaning of Magdalene may have searched for a town with a similar root word. They apparently fixed their attention on the site of Magdala Nunuyah, allegedly destroyed for its iniquity and prostitution or idolatry, and embraced the restored Magdala or Mejdal, rationalizing it as the hometown of Mary Magdalene. Modern-day visitors still swarm to this site on the Sea of Galilee and muse about the sinful life of Mary Magdalene, which it turns out was an unsubstantiated slander.

How could this town be the birthplace of Mary called the Magdalene whom Church fathers—Tertullian, Ambrose, Jerome, Augustine, Bernard, and Thomas Aquinas among them—in their writings universally name as the sister of Lazarus from the town of Bethany?[16]

Medieval chroniclers of the lives of the saints, duped by the Church-fostered tradition of her sullied reputation, often claim that Mary Magdalene's family owned property in both towns, Bethany and Magdala. To their mind, this was the most logical solution for her apparently dual citizenship, and it attempted to reconcile disparate accounts of the anointing in Luke and Mark/John. A notable Latin text formerly attributed to Rabanus Maurus, a ninth-century archbishop of Mainz who wrote sermons about Mary Magdalene, makes that assumption. [17] The book, entitled *Rabanus de Vita Mariae Magdalenae* (Rabanus's Life of Mary Magdalene), dates from about 1408 and is housed in the Magdalen College Library at Oxford. Like most medieval chroniclers, the author of this text erroneously attributed to Rabanus assumes that Mary was the sister of Martha and Lazarus and tells the story of the siblings and their voyage to Gaul. Western Christians did not equivocate on that issue until the Reformation, and even then dissent was muted, although the liturgy for Mary Magdalene's feast day was deleted from the Anglican Book of Common Prayer in the middle of the sixteenth century. Most European artists continued to depict Mary Magdalene with her traditional alabaster jar of ointment in spite of attempts to revise her story and separate her from the sister of Lazarus, who anointed Jesus in John 12:3.

H Magdalhnh

Correctly interpreting the epithet the Magdalene poses several difficulties. If Mary had been a denizen of Magdala, a more likely Greek spelling of her title would have been h Magdalaia, the *aia* ending denoting a woman from a town called Magdala. The *hnh* ending in Greek can mean "daughter of" and is occasionally applied to a Greek city name to designate a female citizen (i.e., Cyzikhnh means "a woman of Cyzikos"), so the standard interpretation remains a possibility. Some scholars consider the *ene* (Greek *hnh*) ending a Latinized form, which is a less likely hypothesis because Mary's honorific is Greek, not Latin—η Μαγδαληνη—in all four gospels at a time when Greek, not Latin, was the *lingua franca* of the eastern provinces of the empire. Given that the gospels themselves were written in Greek, not Latin, the *hnh* suffix was more likely Greek. But why would anyone add a gender-specific Greek suffix to the Aramaic name of a town—especially if a Greek name was currently in use for the same town? Mary could have been called the Tarichhnh or Taricheaia. Something feels fishy about connecting Mary with the town called the Tower of the Fishermen. Encountering the later Aramaic name for the town, Christians who called Jesus the Fish, Ιχθυς, may have concluded that this was the most suitable birthplace for Mary because of its meaning—and so the tradition was born that, for the same reason, appealed to later generations and was perpetuated. The entire rationale woven around the town of Magdala is, in my opinion, a red herring designed to place Mary the Magdalene (the exalted and great one!) as far away as possible from Bethany and the Mount of Olives (of prophetic importance) and to deliberately associate her with a town of evil reputation for prostitution, immorality, or idolatry, or all three.

The Roman Catholic Church continued to maintain the connection of Magdalene with the siblings in Bethany after post-Reformation Bible scholarship, conforming to the Eastern Orthodox tradition, began to separate the two Marys. Only in 1969, in an attempt (misguided, in my view) to adopt a more ecumenical position, did the Catholic Church separate the two Marys—Magdalene and the sister of Lazarus—in official liturgies, providing grounds for modern scholars to label as error the belief that Mary of Bethany and Mary Magdalene were the same person.

The Eastern Orthodox Christians consistently kept Mary Magdalene separate from the Mary who anointed Jesus. They followed the suggestion made by Hippolytus of Rome in his commentary on the Canticle that Mary Magdalene was an apostle: "Eve has become an Apostle." A powerful voice in support of this view was John Chrysostom (347–407), the archbishop of Constantinople. This prelate, born in Antioch, followed the lead of second-century Christians in Syria who had tried to insist that the Virgin Mary be added to the three women who brought ointments and spices to the garden and were witnesses to the empty tomb. John Chrysostom believed that the Virgin was the primary witness to the resurrection and the Eastern Church maintained that distortion of the canonical gospels, raising the status of the Virgin Mother and, by implication, denigrating that of the Magdalene. Their efforts culminated in the proclamation of the Virgin Mary as Theotokos (God-bearer) at the Council of Ephesus in 431 and the epithet "ever Virgin" at the Council of Chalcedon in 451. Meanwhile, Christians in Western Europe continued to honor Mary Magdalene as bride, the personification and bearer of ekklesia, the Church. Could the Eastern prelates, in their zeal to give proper honor to the Blessed Mother, have failed to identify the preeminent Mary in the gospels? A legend not supported by the gospels reflects their theology: Christ is alleged to have appeared to his mother in a special visitation on Holy Saturday, the day before his encounter with Mary Magdalene in the garden. Born of their adulation of the Great Mother, the status of the bride was gradually eroded by those Church fathers intent on writing her out of the Christian story. But when truth is denied, consequences ensue.

Watchtower of the Flock

I am convinced that the earliest Christians were justified in believing that Mary Magdalene and Mary of Bethany were the same woman— bride and beloved of the Davidic Messiah of the Jewish nation. Another rationale easily accounts for Mary's unusual title, a rationale that has no connection to the town called Magdala, allegedly destroyed like Sodom and Gomorrah for its sins of the flesh. Instead, the origin of the title is a potent prophecy of the bride of the sacrificed king. Regrettably, scripture exegetes have for centuries overlooked the explanation precisely because they never recognized Mary Magdalene as the forgotten bride of Christian mythology. The earliest Christians spoke Koiné, a Greek dialect that was lingua franca of the Roman Empire in the East, but they were Jewish, and their preferred language was Aramaic, so perhaps we should look to Hebrew and Aramaic sources, rather than Greek, for the meaning of Mary's honorific.

Among the sacred texts of the Hebrew Bible, deep in the book of the prophet Micah, an obscure passage addresses the bereaved bride, who represents the people of Jerusalem. She is called Daughter of

Zion and is referred to symbolically as the Magdal-eder—the "watchtower" or "stronghold of the flock"—and she mourns the loss of her deceased king:

> *And to you, O Magdal-eder,*
> *Watchtower of the Flock,*
> *stronghold of the Daughter of Sion*
> *unto you shall the former dominion be restored,*
> *the kingdom of daughter Jerusalem.*
> *Now why do you cry?*
> *Have you no king? Has your counselor perished,*
> *that you are seized with pains like a woman in labor? . . .*
> *For now shall you go forth from the city*
> *And dwell in the open fields.*
> *To Babylon shall you go,*
> *and from there you shall be rescued . . .*
> *Now also many nations are gathered against you, that say,*
> *"Let her be defiled . . ."*
>
> MICAH 4:8–11

This passage, written in the eighth century B.C., presents the exact scenario that becomes Mary Magdalene's own story, closely linked with the exile—the Diaspora—of her people. The prophet Micah describes the desolate bride crying over her deceased bridegroom king. He prophesies her foreign exile—and her eventual return!—but he also confirms her denigrated status: "Let her be defiled." One translation of this line calls her "unclean"[18] and another uses "profaned."[19] How can scripture scholars have failed for two millennia to recognize in this prophetic passage the Magdalene in her role as Daughter of Zion—the profaned and denigrated bride of Jesus forced into exile? Why does she cry? Has she no king? Has her *rabboni*—her master and teacher, her "counselor"—perished?

Only a few lines further on in Micah's prophecy, we find a prophetic passage quoted by early Christian exegetes to affirm the claim that the Davidic Messiah would be born in Bethlehem (Micah 5:1). The author of Matthew eagerly included that prophecy in his own text

(Matthew 2:6), showing that Jesus fulfilled the words of the prophet. I believe this earlier passage of Micah 4:8–11 describing the disconsolate bride, the Daughter of Zion, was in a similar way recognized and cited as a prophecy about the bereaved bride of the Christian story, the bride already safely hidden in foreign exile, probably in Gaul, by the time the gospels were committed to papyrus. I am confident that the earliest Christians—those persecuted by Saul and his peers in the Jerusalem Church—knew the words of their prophets and seized upon this passage as an utterance concerning the fate of the bride of their martyred Messiah, just as they seized on passages from Isaiah and the Psalmist as prophecies about events in the life of Jesus. On this basis, they coined the honorific title h Magdalhnh for Mary, tantamount to calling her the Great or the Magnificent. Clearly, they could not call her the wife of Jesus without increasing the risk that Roman authorities would seek to destroy her and her possible descendants as they did others of the *desposyni,* the blood relatives of Jesus and his brothers.

On the basis of the Aramaic root word *magdala,* some suggest that Mary was unusually tall for a woman of her time and ethnic background. The various possible meanings of her epithet are not mutually exclusive; each gives us new insight into the real Mary Magdalene we seek. Another possibility—to my knowledge never mentioned by today's scholars—is that the Hebrew particle *hnh,* used as an interjection to add emphasis by both Amos and Isaiah in their prophetic utterances, was applied to her title by the Jewish community who knew her best. The syllable *hnh* comes from the Hebrew word *hinneh,* abbreviated without vowels. It means "behold!" in the sense of "Look, something new and important is happening!"[20] Perhaps her Jewish friends created a powerful honorific for Mary in their own language—"behold the tower"—a title retained in sacred texts of Christianity, but whose meaning was sadly lost because they did not recognize the Magdal-eder—the desolate bride mourning her fallen king and counselor. In Hebrew, the word *rabbi* is used for "husband" as well as "teacher," and *rabboni,* in John 20:16, when Mary Magdalene recognized the risen Christ in the garden, was a more intense form of the same word.

The Weeping Madonna

The prophetic connection of Mary Magdalene with the bereaved Daughter of Sion is too powerful to be ignored. In Micah 4:9, as always, the disconsolate bride is crying. The ubiquitous and predictable role of the bride and her women companions is to lament the deceased beloved. Ishtar mourns her consort Tammuz in Babylonian mythology, as Isis cries over Osiris and Venus for Adonis. In Ezekiel 8:14, the prophet sees the women of Jerusalem crying over Tammuz, and in Luke 23:28, Jesus admonishes the women of Jerusalem not to weep for him. In John's gospel, Mary Magdalene stands weeping outside the garden tomb. As she weeps, she stoops to look into the sepulcher. Two men seated in the tomb ask her why she is crying, and a short time later, when she encounters the risen Lord and at first mistakes him for the gardener, he too asks her why she is crying. This lament of the bride over the sacrificed bridegroom is the duty and prerogative of the sister-bride from ancient liturgies of the sacrificed king—reflected in the cults of Tammuz, Osiris, Ba'al, Attis, Adonis, and other tortured and sacrificed pagan gods whose bride mourns the death of her mutilated mate. This is the "never-ending story" that is repeated in Micah 4, when the Daughter of Sion mourns her perished king and counselor, and that is once again re-enacted at the tomb of Jesus.

In fact, tears are a distinguishing feature of the Mary called the Magdalene. In John's gospel, she cries over the death of her brother Lazarus, moving Jesus with her tears: ". . . he groaned in spirit and was troubled" (John 11:33). She later cries over the feet of Jesus and wipes them with her own hair (John 12:3). She cries for her king and counselor (her rabbi) in Micah's prophecy (4:8) and at the tomb (John 20:11). She cries again in the gnostic Gospel of Mary, when Peter rejects her testimony about a vision of the risen Christ. And ubiquitously in Christian art, she weeps. The sorrowful Madonna who cries in the passages of the New Testament is not the mother of Jesus, but rather his bride. At the Basilica of the Madeleine at Vézelay, an oversized statue of Mary Magdalene stands in a side chapel—majestic, yet graceful—cradling the Grail chalice against her abdomen, as a woman sometimes cradles her unborn child (plate 8). The statue, sculpted by Desvergnes in 1924, has a tear on her cheek, a poignant reminder of her role as the bereaved bride weeping for her deceased beloved. At some point in my search, I began to wonder if the statues of the Madonna who cries in so many shrines and churches around the world might represent Mary Magdalene—whose tears are a ubiquitous and distinctive characteristic of her iconography. The English word *maudlin* is derived from the French spelling of her name (Madeleine) and means "overly sentimental" or "emotional." To the extent that Madonna images represent the feminine face of God and its manifestation in the emotional feminine half of creation, tears are hers.

Goddess of Wisdom

Although the ending *hnh* attached to the tower/fortress (magdala) has been claimed, mistakenly in my opinion, to identify Mary as a resident of a town called Magdala, yet another plausible explanation exists for this suffix and its appeal to a Greek-speaking audience. To many, the *hnh* was already familiar in connection with the patroness of Athens, the goddess Athena (in Greek, Αθηνη). The connection between Athena and Mary Magdalene is reinforced by a ritual practiced in the cult of the goddess in her holy city. Caitlín Matthews describes the ceremony in her book *Sophia, Goddess of Wisdom*. Relying on research into the cult of Athena done by the Hungarian scholar Karoly Kerényi, Matthews describes a ritual celebrating the dark aspect of the goddess as an endangered and exiled deity whose priestess in ancient times may have been offered as a human sacrifice.[21] During rituals celebrating the ominous day of her trial and suffering, the priestess—originally called Agraulos—was festooned with ornaments and sent out to undergo her ordeal, spending the night in the open fields to reenact her descent into darkness. Matthews notes that these rites appear to presage the suffering and descent (exile) of the gnostic Sophia.

I find it amazing that Matthews's book, published in 1991, which includes a remarkable depth of information about the ancient goddesses and about the rites of sacred marriage, makes no mention of Mary Magadalene! The Agraulos rites of Athena echo in precise language Micah's prophecy of the Magdal-eder, the stronghold of the Daughter of Zion: "[F]or now shall you go forth . . . and dwell in the open fields" (Micah 4:10). If these rites of Athena's cult foreshadow the descent and exile, denigration, and defilement of Sophia, then they are most certainly related to the dark aspect of the Christian goddess of wisdom as well—incarnate in the Mary called Magdalene. We will examine the Sophia myth more fully in the next chapter.

Associations with this goddess of wisdom may have been considered when deciding on the title h Magdalhnh, keeping in mind that the sacred sum of the values of the letters (gematria) was of supreme importance when coining names and honorifics. Just as the Greek spelling of Ihsous (Yeshua in Hebrew) was coined to maximize its symbolic impact by gematria, Magdalene's sacred number by gematria had to reflect the cosmic principle she embodied. The sum of Ihsous was 888, the principle of resurrection and regeneration, while 153, the sum of h Magdalhnh, was associated with the womb, the matrix, the cauldron of creativity, and the "vessel of the fish."[22] These symbols have obvious feminine connotations and were universally associated with the goddesses of wisdom and fertility in the ancient Near East. Only when the article *h* is included does the sum of her title h Magdalhnh provide the all-important identification with the Great Goddess of the ancient world. Whoever attached this honorific title to Mary did it deliberately to ensure universal recognition of her status as First Lady among those who had "eyes to see."

Recently, Joan Beth Clair, an artist in California, sent me a beautiful poem and painting she said was inspired by Mary Magdalene (plate 9). She calls her painting *Alive in Her*. For me, this extraordinary picture illustrates without words the nameless obscurity of the lost bride, an archetype so buried in our consciousness that we can barely envision her! The figure in the painting echoes the *vesica piscis* [◊] symbol of the Goddess and has deep connections with vines and spirals denoting women's wisdom of the earth and blood mysteries of female fecundity, but also of spiritual wisdom represented by stylized origami birds. The beautiful and evocative image of the archetypal bride has no face.

Family Ties

There is no proof that the woman metaphorically called the Tower or Stronghold of the Flock was of Benjaminite origin, but strongly suggestive evidence favors that theory. Magdal, the Tower or Watchtower, also means "stronghold," "fortress," "citadel," or "bulwark," implying walls built to protect the people of the city. The first mention of the Magdal-eder is found not in Micah but in Genesis. It is a hill located not far from the town of Bethlehem, used by local shepherds as a vantage point while tending their sheep. It may well have been the hillock where the shepherds in Luke's gospel received the message of the nativity from angel choirs. Rachel, the beloved wife of Jacob, died giving birth to Benjamin and her grieving husband buried her near Bethlehem. The extended family of the patriarch of Israel then moved on beyond the Magdal-eder, which was probably located between Bethlehem and Hebron, and made camp there (Genesis 35:21). This passage connects the tomb of Rachel, mother of Benjamin, with the neighborhood of the Magdal-eder. Traditional territories later assigned to the tribe of Benjamin included the region surrounding Jerusalem, possibly because his mother, Rachel, was buried in the vicinity. The archaeologist W. F. Albright identified Bethany with Ananyab, in an area inhabited by the tribe of Benjamin after their return from exile in Babylon (Nehemiah 11:32).

The family of siblings who owned property in Bethany, then, were probably Benjaminite. A further passage found in Genesis tells the story of the eleven sons of Jacob and their reunion with their brother Joseph, whom the elder brothers had sold into slavery. The catalyst for their reunion is the cup found in Benjamin's sack—symbolically prophetic of the Grail—because the chalice or cup is an archetypal symbol for the feminine. The cup or bride from the tribe of Benjamin thus has the potential to bring about the reconciliation and "healing of the nations," just as the Grail has restorative healing properties when it is returned to the wounded king.

If a daughter from the tribe of Benjamin was in truth the spouse and beloved of Jesus, the Davidic Messiah, their dynastic union would have had powerful political and prophetic ramifications in their

Roman-occupied country. In fact, their marriage might well have been kept a closely guarded secret for that reason—to protect them and their heirs from Roman retribution.

What is the gospel account of the anointing really saying? Was the anointing of Jesus by the woman from Bethany actually a marriage rite? Was she the bride of ancient mythology who mourned the fallen bridegroom and was reunited with him in the garden? Was the sacred union of the beloveds at the heart of the Christian proclamation of the good news? Was it designed to be the birthright of future generations of Christians to honor the Divine incarnate in the Christ couple of the Christian mythology? We have no marriage certificate for Jesus and Mary, but the evidence is strong. Clearly their mandala for sacred partnership was broken very early in the cradle of Christianity. But the record of its presence is retained in the gospels for anyone who has "eyes to see." Some of Jesus' teachings were understood only by the initiated and the inner circle of his friends, and even these often missed the message. Where is the evidence that the sacred union was at the heart of the story from the beginning? Whom can we quote?

Over and over in the New Testament, we encounter stories and parables referring to the bridegroom. John the Baptist attests to the role of his cousin Jesus as bridegroom of Israel: "He who has the bride is the bridegroom; but the friend of the bridegroom, who stands and hears him, rejoices exceedingly at the voice of the bridegroom. This my joy, therefore, is made full" (John 3:29). Jesus styles himself as the bridegroom who departs and the Kingdom of God as a wedding feast. He proceeds to tell the story of a king who held a marriage banquet for his son, but the guests found excuses to avoid attending (Matthew 22:1–10). Perhaps Jesus understood his own ministry and vision as a similar wedding feast—an egalitarian honoring of the feminine and the symbiosis of partnership—to which all were invited, but many refused to come. Perhaps the sacred union was the cornerstone the builders rejected. Many people rejected it in the first century. And many reject it still. Clearly the Roman-dominated world of the first century was not ready to embrace the gospel of gender equality and inclusiveness, but the seed of this radical doctrine was planted at the very heart of the story—the seed of the Kingdom of God, both within and around us, and in our midst.

A further piece of scriptural evidence in favor of the sacred marriage as the preeminent model for Christian community is found in the parable of the mustard seed. This familiar seed mentioned in the three synoptic gospels, as well as in the gnostic Gospel of Thomas, is a metaphor for the kingdom of heaven. Based on its illuminating gematria, the mustard seed (1746) is associated with fusion in Plato's *Timaeus*.[23] For the Pythagorean philosophers, the symbolic number represented the fertilized ovum or sacred seed—the symbiotic union of masculine and feminine polarities. Thus, the mustard-seed metaphor depicts the Kingdom of God as the sacred union of masculine (666) and feminine (1080) energies in a symbiotic and harmonious whole, similar to the concept of integration of Logos and Eros in Jungian terminology. The Kingdom of God (already in our midst) is identified in the mustard-seed parable as the sacred marriage itself, an archetypal mandala for life abundant, the life of mutuality, of generous service and self-giving modeled by Christ and his beloved, an example of loving partnership adopted by his brothers and other disciples of the Way, traveling with their own sister-wives as they spread the gospel throughout the Mediterranean world.

So what happened? If that was the model indigenous to Christianity, how did we manage to lose the bride? Was her story too dangerous to be spoken aloud? She has been stricken from the orthodox version of the story by the fourth century, stripped of her robes and titles and sent—like Hagar, the bondwoman of Abraham and Sarah—into desert exile.

And from there she shall be rescued.

4

Sophia, Spouse of the Lord

*I bud forth delights like the vine, my blossoms become
fruit fair and rich. Come to me, all you that yearn for
me, and be filled with my fruits; you will remember me
as sweeter than honey, better than the honeycomb.*

SIRACH 24:17–19

On a sunny December afternoon in 1945, three brothers were gathering
soft dirt from a remote cliff side in their native Egypt when one of the
brothers, an Arab peasant named Muhammed 'Ali al-Sammān, unex-
pectedly struck something hard in the earth. In growing astonishment,
he excavated the object, a large red earthenware jar nearly six feet in
height, buried in the sandy soil. When he broke it open, Muhammed
was at first dismayed to see that the jar contained leather-bound papyrus
books of obvious antiquity. Overcoming his disappointment and sensing
the possible value of his find, he and his brothers trundled the thirteen
antique books back to their village. So begins a remarkable modern-day
saga—the rescue, retrieval, and eventual revelation of a gnostic library, a
body of literature buried in the late fourth century in a dry riverbed near
the Egyptian town of Nag Hammadi by unnamed monks eager to save
the teachings of their persecuted sect. Scholars speculate that the codices
might have been interred following a ban placed on them by Athanasius,
the Christian archbishop of Alexandria, in 367. Another possibility is

70

that the documents were hidden several decades earlier to protect them from destruction by Monophysites, a sect of Christians who claimed that Jesus had only divine nature, not physical.[1] Following instructions given to the Hebrew prophet Jeremiah to preserve a document in an earthenware jar, enterprising monks hid the thirteen most valuable books from their library in the clay jar, and the isolated desert terrain successfully preserved the documents for nearly sixteen hundred years.

Since the accidental discovery of this literary treasure in 1945, scholars have been poring over the documents, translating and interpreting the difficult—often damaged—texts, eagerly searching their depths for the wisdom of gnostic sectarians driven out of Christian congregations by stern decrees of the orthodox priests and bishops who declared the gnostic teachings heretical. These recovered codices have been invaluable, casting new light on the diverse beliefs and the struggles of early Christians to establish creeds that could be held in common by the entire community of believers. Whereas orthodox priests insisted that belief in Jesus, baptism in his name, and obedience to his priests was sufficient for salvation, gnostics believed that salvation was a soul's journey toward spiritual enlightenment under the direct inspiration and guidance of the risen Jesus Christ, through the action of the Holy Spirit. For these sectarians, the goal of the Christian was to encounter the Christ on a spiritual plane rather than to profess belief in a memorized creed. Struggles over doctrines of Christology and interpretation of scripture continued for more than three centuries in Egypt and the Middle East before gnostic sects were officially forced out of mainstream Christianity and into exile, relentlessly driven out by neighbors who cast rocks at them as they fled.

The collected wisdom of one monastic community was bound into leather covers and hidden in the red clay jar at the foot of the Jabal al-Tarif. Their voices were silenced and their teachings eventually sank into the desert sands and were channeled into an underground stream, later reemerging in Western Europe to water the seeds of the Renaissance—nurturing the rebirth of an ancient wisdom tradition after long centuries of exile. In the interim years, we must rely on the polemic of their adversaries for hints about the tenets of their faith.

One allegation leveled against gnostic Christians was that they relied on numbers theology to interpret scripture, supporting the theory that gnostic sectarians were aware of the universal wisdom of the Pythagorean School of philosophy. Initiates of the schools studied secret doctrines, including the canons of sacred geometry that expressed cosmic principles as numbers. Powerful evidence of Pythagorean influence is found in the gematria of classic literature and of Judeo-Christian sacred texts. A few New Testament scholars are now addressing the issue of symbolic numbers found in scripture and their astonishing implications. Unfortunately for the integrity of New Testament scholarship, a number of Christians, even in our enlightened age, attack this fascinating field of study, giving it a negative spin by branding it "numerology." Gematria is not numerology and is not used for divination. It is, rather, a historically verified literary device used to enhance the impact of a name or phrase by deliberate association with the symbolic number of the cosmic principle it manifests. Both Hebrew and Greek alphabets attach numeric values to each letter, and both the Hebrew Bible and the Greek New Testament—gospels, Epistles, and Book of Revelation—are replete with phrases enhanced by gematria.[2] Instead of setting the passages of their most important sacred texts to music, our ancestors set them to number.

Magdalene, Favorite Disciple

For scholars studying the long-hidden gnostic texts, one of the most startling revelations of the Nag Hammadi library has been the high esteem in which Mary called the Magdalene was held among adherents of several persecuted sects who authored the rejected gospels and treatises. Hints of the honor in which Mary Magdalene was held among early communities of Christians first surfaced in the late nineteenth century with the publication of the gnostic Gospel of Mary and a Valentinian gnostic text entitled Pistis Sophia. Devalued and vilified in a Western European tradition that branded her a prostitute, the preeminent female saint emerges from these and several other gnostic documents as the favored and most beloved of all the disciples of Jesus, his closest and dearest companion, and even his consort and counter-part. Although only a few gnostic texts mention Mary Magdalene at all, none associates her with a common harlot or prostitute. Instead, she is characterized as the favorite disciple of the Lord and, in one gospel, as his intimate companion. In several of the suppressed texts, the male disciples and apostles are clearly jealous of Jesus' intimacy with Mary Magdalene; they cannot understand why the Lord would share esoteric teachings with her that he did not share with them.

This resentful attitude of the male apostles toward Mary Magdalene reflects the prevailing mind-set of their late-second- and third-century milieu—the belief that men were important citizens and that women existed to serve men in a role that was inferior. In a notable passage found near the end of the gnostic Gospel of Thomas, Jesus states that he will make Mary an *anthropos*. Sadly, the Greek word *anthropos* in this text has been widely misunderstood to mean "male," though it might be more accurately translated as "perfected human being," in the sense of a complete or realized, fully human person.[3] In this passage, Jesus promises not to make Mary masculine in gender, but rather to transform her into a perfected spiritual being whose gender is irrelevant. In his time and milieu—first-century Judaism where men and women worshipped in separate venues and men thanked God during morning devotions that they were not "born a woman"—the mere idea of a woman as a spiritual being equal to a man was a radical departure from convention, but it was one of the hallmarks of early Christianity.

We cannot tell for certain whether the gnostic texts reflect accurately a tradition of physical intimacy between Jesus and Mary Magdalene and his preference for her over his other apostles, but the tradition itself is irrefutable, based squarely on the witness of the canonical gospels that style the two as beloveds. We have only to consider their repeated testimony that Mary Magdalene was more faithful to Jesus than were Peter and the other male apostles named as the twelve. She remains near Jesus throughout his agony on the cross. She is present at his deposition and interment and present again in the garden on Easter morning, where she comes as a close family member to perform the ritual anointing of the deceased, along with his mother and aunt (or sister) Salome (Mark 16:1). Perhaps the gnostic texts extolling her spiritual enlightenment merely reflect this universally accepted tradition of Mary Magdalene's ardent devotion to Jesus, which earned her the unique privilege of first witness to the resurrection. On this basis alone, proclaiming her the beloved or favorite disciple would be justified.

The Companion of the Savior

The gnostic Gospel of Philip carries testimony of the special relationship between Jesus and the Magdalene much further, attesting to a relationship of surprising intensity—of which the male disciples were demonstrably jealous: "The partner of the Savior is Mary Magdalene."[4] The Greek/Coptic *koinōnos* can also be translated as "spouse," "consort," or "companion" as well as "partner."

On several occasions in the suppressed texts, Peter complains that Mary Magdalene appears to have received special, secret teachings from Jesus. In the Gospel of Mary, Peter is rebuffed by Levi, who defends Mary: "Yet if the Teacher found her worthy, who are you to reject her?"[5] Levi continues, asserting that Jesus "knew her very well, for he loved her more than us." In examining these texts, we find the two major protagonists, Peter and Mary, represent two distinct approaches to the good news of the Christian story. While Peter grasps the fundamental tenets of the life, death, and resurrection of Jesus, holding them as historical facts of which he is the designated chief guardian, Mary is in constant communion with the risen Christ—the recipient of ongoing revelation directly communicated heart to heart: "[F]or it was in silence that the Teacher spoke to her."[6]

The third-century text of the Gospel of Philip refers to Mary Magdalene as the koinōnos—the intimate companion or consort—of the Savior and goes on to relate that the apostles were jealous or disapproving of her because Jesus kissed her often. Although the text is damaged so that we cannot determine exactly where Jesus kissed her— whether on the cheek, forehead, lips, or shoulder—the text implies that he kissed her on the mouth, because the other apostles were affronted by this frequent intimacy. They ask Jesus why he loves Mary more than he does them and his answer implies that they are spiritually dense while Mary is enlightened. Obviously, from statements found in this gospel and in the gnostic tract Pistis Sophia, Mary is seen as the most spiritually enlightened of the disciples surrounding the Savior. Surprisingly, she is not called the Magdalene in any of the gnostic gospels except in the Gospel of Philip. The woman referred to as the "other Mary" is identified as the mother of Jesus, and Mary Magdalene is simply called Maria or Miriam and "the blessed one."

In the celebrated passage from the Gospel of Philip expressing the intimacy of Jesus with Mary Magdalene, we hear a distinct refrain from the opening lines of the Hebrew Song of Songs: "Let him kiss me with the kisses of his mouth" (Song of Songs 1:1). The bride in the Song then requests the king to take her to his chambers, which may have influenced later gnostic views on the sacrament of the bridal chamber. The Song of Songs was interpreted as an extended metaphor for God's love for his bride, the people of Israel, and later, by Christians, as one expressing Christ's love for his Church. One of my strongest convictions is that the sacred union celebrated in the Song of Songs was integral to understanding the early Christians, modeled by Jesus and Mary Magdalene and the foundation of their egalitarian worldview in which women shared fully with men in community life. The sacred union is not only spiritual and mystic relationship, but one that manifests at all levels of existence as well. The ultimate union of flesh and divinity occurs in the "temple of the Holy Spirit"—each human person.

Because a kiss suggests a sharing of breath, a kiss unites two people in an intimacy both physical and spiritual. Jean-Yves Leloup, a mystic and scholar who has translated several gnostic gospels, including the Gospel of Philip and the Gospel of Mary, suggests that the body of gnostic literature buried near Nag Hammadi was hidden to protect it from destruction precisely because it portrayed physical intimacy between Jesus and Mary Magdalene, culminating in the bridal chamber of sexual union.[7] The physical nature of Jesus was attacked by Docetic and Monophysite sects whose adherents denied Jesus' full humanity, holding that he was a purely spiritual being, while the orthodox insisted that Jesus came in the flesh, declaring, "Every spirit that confesses that Jesus Christ has come in the flesh is of God" (1 John 4:2). Mainstream Christians believed in an actual, historical, and very human Jesus whose legacy of teachings they celebrated, "like unto us in all things but sin."

The issue of Jesus' full humanity is clearly stated in the Gospel of Philip, where the Savior is uniquely presented as the seed of Joseph the Carpenter, [8] a statement that ignores any hint of the virgin birth but acknowledges the genealogical passages found in Matthew and Luke that Jesus was the son of Joseph. According to the inspired analysis of Jean-Yves Leloup, the Gospel of Philip is not just about the holiness of spiritual communion; rather it expresses the sacred nature of the physical union of a man and woman, the mystery of the bridal chamber, as an expression of God's presence. The author of this apocryphal gospel calls Mary Magdalene the koinōnos of Jesus and later in the text uses a word derived from the same root, *koinōnia,* translated as "mating."[9] Although other biblical texts, including the canonical epistles in the New Testament, translate the word *koinōnos* to mean "companion," in the sense of a friend, the word carries a more intimate meaning, with sexual connotations, for the author of the Gospel of Philip. Leloup apparently feels that the central theme of this gospel was the full humanity of Jesus and that his intimacy with Mary Magdalene was an expression and proof of this fullness.[10] Leloup suggests that a primary theme of the Gospel of Philip is "the union of man and woman as revelation of the Love of creator and savior."[11] Further, he maintains that the sexual act belongs to the divine realm—a "theophany," or revelation, of God.[12] For Leloup, these themes in the Gospel of Philip reflect long-held Jewish traditions about the holiness of sex and procreation and the complementary essence of masculine and feminine. Among apocryphal texts of gnostics who allegedly denied the flesh and viewed the physical world as the corrupt creation of an inferior god they called the Demiurge, the Gospel of Philip, with its emphasis on the holiness of the marriage act, appears to be an anomaly.

The Gospel of Mary

The Gospel of Mary is a gnostic document also found in Egypt although not among the thirteen gnostic codices discovered in the jar buried near Nag Hammadi. In this second-century text, sadly damaged such that the first several pages are missing, Magdalene continues to receive revelation from visions and locutions of the risen Christ long after his resurrection. Her experience is similar to traditional modes of mystics worldwide who relate to the Divine through dreams, visions, altered consciousness, and other spiritual encounters. Hers is not a rigid faith based on memorized creeds; it is one of direct experiential relationship with the Savior. Because Mary receives inspiration and consolation from the risen Christ, she attempts to comfort and encourage the male apostles, who are reluctant to accept her testimony. Finally, Mary begins to weep. As we have noted, crying is one of Mary Magdalene's distinct roles in the canonical scriptures, expressive of her deep well of emotions. She is wounded when Peter scorns her way of experiencing Jesus in visionary encounters. Through her tears, she asks Peter if he thinks she imagined her experiences. In a world that honors the rational Logos or left-brain knowledge—scientifically proved, historically accurate, and concrete—Mary, embodiment of the right-brained artist/mystic/visionary, is ridiculed and eventually silenced by the apostle who, by virtue of his name, is associated with the Rock—the rigid, legalistic, and unsympathetic patriarchal Peter.

The evident rivalry between Peter's way and Mary's is rooted in the psychology of masculine and feminine and in the dualism of left-brain, right-handed or Logos orientation in opposition to right-brain, left-handed intuitive ways of relating to reality. Peter, the Rock, represents the orthodox version of Christianity, the vessel or bark of Christians who memorize creeds and catechisms and are awarded safe passage to paradise through the mediation of hierarchical priests with absolute authority over their lives and souls, to whom they owe honor and strict obedience. Mary's is the way of the heart—compassionate relationship with the Divine and with creation. In doctrines of the orthodox, Peter holds the keys of the kingdom. What he binds on earth is bound in heaven. These familiar tenets of institutional Christianity are derived from passages in the canonical gospels originally accepted by Bishop

Irenaeus and later Church fathers in the third and fourth centuries. The patriarchs concluded that these contained authentic teachings of Jesus, based on what they believed to be eyewitness testimony of two apostles—Matthew and John—and of two other authors, Mark and Luke, who they believed were direct disciples of Peter and Paul, respectively. Modern scholarship has determined that, in all probability, not one of the accepted gospels was written by an eyewitness, but among early Christians, the four gospels were widely accepted as authentic accounts of Jesus' life and ministry. Delegations of priests later created the Christian creeds and established doctrines accepted at various church councils during the early Christian era, gradually solidifying and institutionalizing what had begun as a spontaneous movement honoring the memory of the charismatic rabbi Yeshua, his wisdom teachings, and his Way of reconciliation.

In choosing from numerous texts emerging out of diverse Christian communities those that they found doctrinally acceptable, the founding fathers of the institutional Church—the guardians of the walls—gradually silenced the voice of Mary Magdalene and of the ardent followers of her way of the heart. Her devotees, gnostic sectarians who claimed they received their teachings directly from her, honored and encouraged the faith journey of each soul in its search for enlightenment and mystical union with the Divine. Some diverse groups of early Christians apparently understood the basic tenets of Christianity as allegory or mythology rather than as literal, historical fact.

Mary and the Sophia

An important legacy of the gnostic view of Mary Magdalene is their image of her as the human incarnation of the Sophia, or Feminine Consciousness. Citizens of the power-drunk Roman Empire—both Jewish and Gentile philosophers—saw that the honor once paid to the goddess Wisdom/Sophia had been superseded by solar and warrior cults of the gods Apollo and Mithras, as well as by various forms of emperor worship. In The Wisdom of Solomon, a text written in the first century in Alexandria, Wisdom (Sophia) is characterized as the "spouse of the

Lord," the mirror of God's energy and emanation of God's glory, a concept similar to the Jewish articulation of the Shekinah, the feminine manifestation or presence of the glory of God. The philosophers, literally the "lovers of Sophia," lamented that the virtues of Wisdom (often synonymous with the Holy Spirit) were so universally spurned. In the Wisdom books of the Hebrew Bible, the Sophia hawked her wares in the streets, but few were interested. She had fallen into ill repute, her precepts widely scorned—so, too, her human daughters were devalued and abused, as in the story of Eve and her alleged disobedience in the Garden of Eden that stigmatized her daughters. As in the Genesis story, the fate of Wisdom/Sophia was the story not of one woman, but rather of all women, seen as inferior to men from birth. In Magdalene, they witnessed the redemption and return of Sophia as the cherished partner and beloved of God.

The calculation of a simple geometric diagram beautifully illustrates the myth of the Sophia and connects her intimately with 153, the sacred number of the Magdalene. A circle represents a person, and the center—the core or bridal chamber of the person—is designated by a dot. A line is drawn from the center to the edge of the circle, creating a radius seven units in length. Seven represents the Holy Spirit or Sophia who has fallen away from her core or "bridal chamber" and descended into the circumference or shell, which represents the flesh and identification with her physical senses.

Recognizing that the gnostics were initiated into Pythagorean geometry and its sacred canons, we can see how this geometric figure connects the story of the fallen Sophia—the soul—with Mary Magdalene. Using the standard Greek ratio 22/7 for pi, the outer circumference of a circle with a radius of 7 is 44, closely associated with 444, the sacred number by gematria of the phrase σαρξ και αιμα (flesh and blood), found in 1 Corinthians 15:50, and associated with matter and the created earth in the Greek canon of sacred number. The area of the same circle representing the Sophia in her descent into the flesh is calculated by multiplying radius squared by pi: $49 \times 22/7 = 154$, synonymous (by virtue of the colel of +1 or −1) with 153, the sacred number of h Magdalhnh, Mary's epithet. A further association of Mary Magdalene with a circle is found in her official feast day on the Roman Catholic calendar of saints, the twenty-second day of the seventh month.

The gospels bear strong witness that Jesus worked to reverse the derogatory view of the feminine and to redeem her during the years of his ministry. In passages unparalleled in contemporary literature, the gospels present Jesus as an emissary of Sophia and champion of abused and abased women. The Samaritan woman at the well, the woman caught in adultery, the unclean woman with the continuous flux, and Peter's mother-in-law all represent the marginalized role of women in Jewish society. Jesus is presented as the redeemer of the fallen and devalued feminine consciousness, most fully embraced in his relationship with Mary Magdalene, whom he allegedly healed of possession by seven demons, metaphorically purifying and restoring the feminine to her rightful status as beloved.

The redemption of the bride echoes a prevalent theme found in the Hebrew Bible. In the book of the prophet Ezekiel, Yahweh chooses Israel as his bride when she is an abandoned child, naked and neglected. When she is later unfaithful to their marriage covenant, he calls her back, forgiving her infidelities. The theme is articulated again in the book of Hosea, when the prophet is instructed to take the prostitute Gomer as his wife and to forgive her recurring betrayals as a sign of Yahweh's love for his people. Recognizing this theme from the Hebrew Scriptures, I think it probable that precisely this connection—the redemption of the land and people as bride and beloved of God—motivated later Christian fathers who styled Mary Magdalene as a repentant prostitute. Hers is not merely the story of one historical woman, but rather the myth of the redemption of each human individual and of the entire community in search of union with the beloved Creator/Redeemer. On the metaphorical level, the story of Mary Magdalene, like the myth of the fallen Sophia, is the story of the soul.

The Gnostic Sophia

The myth of the fallen Sophia was apparently widely promulgated among gnostics and was integral to the story of Mary Magdalene interpreted from the gospel narratives. Gnostic Christians saw the Sophia myth as a metaphor for the soul in each person that, instead of being conscious of its divine origin and true nature centered in the spiritual core, the "bridal chamber" of its being, had somehow fallen away and mistakenly identified itself with its flesh and senses.[13] Having forgotten the divine spark for which it is a vessel or temple, the individual eagerly sought gratification of fleshly desires in excessive self-indulgence, often falling into gross temptations, lusting after the "fleshpots of Egypt," and sinking farther and farther from its spiritual center. The sinful and ignorant person becomes corrupt and spiritually lost, like the prodigal son in the gospel parable.

The myth continues. The soul wanders in exile, succumbing to temptations of the flesh and ultimately becoming disillusioned with her sordid and destructive lifestyle. She begins to feel the alienation from her source—her true spiritual nature—and finally repents her willfulness. In a moment of desperation, she cries out to God for salvation and immediately her bridegroom/brother—the Christ—is sent to rescue her and bring her back to her true self. They unite in the bridal chamber—re-creating the archetypal hieros gamos, or sacred union of Sophia/Logos. This is the story of every soul and its journey toward transformation and reunion—a theme that recurs in several gnostic texts, including the Pistis Sophia and the Hymn of the Pearl. It is metaphorically extended to Mary Magdalene as well.

We can see how, for these gnostic communities, the Magdalene in the canonical gospels embodied the fallen Sophia and how her redemption from Luke's sinful woman to favorite disciple modeled the soul's journey from alienation to union with Christ. Luke's allegation that Mary Magdalene was cured of possession by seven demons is an allusion to her spiritual purification and strongly influenced articulaton of the myth that she was redeemed from a life of prostitution. Over the centuries, this became the prevailing story of Mary Magdalene even for orthodox Christians. She was styled the penitent Sophia redeemed and enjoying intimate spiritual union with the risen Christ.

Magdalene's Spiritual Preeminence

In the Pistis Sophia, probably written in the third century, Mary Magdalene engages in most of the dialogue with Jesus and, by the insightful nature of her questions, establishes that she is the most enlightened of the disciples, earning Jesus' praise for her understanding of his spiritual teachings. "Jesus, the compassionate, answered and said to Mariam, 'Mariam, thou blessed one, whom I will complete in all the mysteries of the height, speak openly, thou art she whose heart is more directed to the Kingdom of Heaven than all thy brothers.' "[14] In contrast, the mother of Jesus, who is also present in this text, is called the other Mary and has markedly lower status than the Magdalene. For modern Christians, this seems an intolerable affront to the Virgin Mary, demoting the woman we have been taught to hold in highest esteem as the Blessed Mother and even Queen of Heaven. It shocks us to find her demoted to the "other Mary." Where could the gnostic author of the Pistis Sophia have gotten this idea, so at odds with our view of the honored status of the Blessed Virgin Mary?

The gnostic tradition of the preeminence of Mary Magdalene at the tomb on Easter morning actually stems from the canonical gospel of Matthew, which places two women at the sepulcher of Jesus on the evening of his entombment and again on Easter morning: "But Mary Magdalene and the other Mary were there, sitting opposite the sepulcher" (Matthew 27:61); " . . . as the first day of the week began to dawn, Mary Magdalene and the other Mary came to see the sepulcher" (Matthew 28:1). This other Mary, the mother of James and Joseph, is sometimes claimed to be Jesus' aunt, the sister of his mother, by Roman Catholic theologians zealous to uphold the tenet of the perpetual virginity of the mother of Jesus. But, as we noted earlier, in reading Mark 6:3 and Matthew 13:55, we conclude that she is the mother of Jesus—and also of James, Joseph, Simon, and Jude, who are clearly identified not as the cousins, but as the brothers of Jesus. The Greek language has a word for "kinsman" that could have been used in this passage, but was not. If Mark, and later Matthew, had wanted to identify these four men as cousins of Jesus, they could have used the word for "cousin" (νεψιοσ) rather than "brother" (δελφος).

Apparently, the gnostics were conscious of the preeminence of Mary Magdalene in the canonical gospels and reflected this scripture-based belief in their own texts. The identity of First Lady in the eyes of the gnostic author of the Pistis Sophia is not in doubt. In this text, Mary Magdalene is called "blessed," she who will "inherit the whole kingdom of the light." Peter disparages Mary Magdalene in this treatise, complaining that she dominates the discussion about the fall of the Sophia so that the male disciples have no opportunity to speak, but Jesus rebukes Peter, upholding the right of Mary and the other women present to speak as inspired by the divine Spirit.

This surprising passage appears to be a political statement by the gnostic author supporting the role of inspired women in the community to preach, teach, and prophesy—roles permitted during the period when Paul's epistles were written (50–65), but denied by Irenaeus and the orthodox Church fathers in the late second century and thereafter. Certain gnostic sects insisted on retaining women in leadership roles in their communities, ostensibly modeled on the discipleship of Mary Magdalene, whose prominence was thoroughly established in the canonical New Testament.

Only once, at the foot of the cross in the fourth gospel, is the mother of Jesus mentioned before Mary Magdalene in the gospels. Later Christian theologians elevated the Virgin to preeminence as the Theotokos (Godbearer) and Mediatrix—an attribute of the Great Mother. But in the texts of the suppressed gnostic communities, Mary Magdalene is invariably recognized as the spiritual partner of Jesus, his intimate companion—the koinōnos whom he loved more than any other woman and more than all his other disciples. This view is irrefutably supported by twin pillars of evidence from the canonical gospels: the mythology of the sacrificed king at the heart of the Christian story; and the gematria of h Magdalhnh, the title of Mary Magdalene. Her sacred number, 153—calculated by adding the letters of her title—equates her symbolically with the 153 fishes in the unbroken net in John 21:11, a metaphor for the Church in the geometry story presented in that chapter.[15] It associates her also with the vesica piscis, the vessel of the fish—an archetypal symbol of the Great Goddess known to Greek geometers as "womb," and "doorway to life."[16] The vesica piscis bears further feminine associations with the bridal chamber and the Holy of Holies.

By insisting on the role of Magdalene as the one most intimately associated with Jesus and his teachings, the gnostics were deliberately upholding the experiential, mystic way of personal encounter with the Divine. In the Apocalypse of Peter, another text from the Nag Hammadi library, some orthodox Christians who called themselves bishop or deacon are characterized as waterless canals. Apparently their gnostic adversaries sensed that the legalistic literalism of the orthodox flowed from an empty well.

Several gnostic texts, especially the Gospel of Mary, bear clear witness to the high esteem in which these suppressed Christian sects held Mary Magdalene and the Way of personal enlightenment for which she was their spokeswoman. On the basis of these long-suppressed documents, feminist Bible scholars eagerly support the supreme status of Mary Magdalene among the apostles of Jesus. Not only is she the messenger first commissioned to carry the good news of the risen Lord, as established in the canonical gospels, but according to texts from the gnostic library, she also endeavors to sustain and comfort the other apostles, confiding to them the secret teachings she has continued to receive in post-resurrection visions of Jesus. In the Gospel of Mary (written c. 120–150), her emotional revelations are received guardedly and with a marked lack of enthusiasm by several apostles, especially Peter, whose resentment mirrors the tension between Church fathers and gnostics whose *gnosis*, or knowledge, of the Divine came through experiential, direct illumination.

Concretizing the Word of God

This tension continues. Today, as in the past, Christian clergy are notably reluctant to accept ecstatic dreams, visions, and channeled messages received by members of their flock, believing that such transmissions are unreliable at best and at worst misleading and heretical. They prefer to confine the communications of the Divine to the word of God already expressed in the Bible. For them, the prophet does not *go* to the mountain to hear the word of God, but rather, the prophet *went* to the mountain, and the revelation received is a sealed book. Do they not muzzle God?

Visionaries over past centuries have received intense scrutiny, and endorsement of their testimony by the Church has been, in most cases, unenthusiastic if not absent. Numerous mystics, prominent among them Hildegard von Bingen and Teresa of Avila, were required to tailor their revelations to fit into the box of ecclesiastic restrictions, often restraining themselves from confiding their visions to their spiritual directors, lest their beliefs be declared false or heretical.

The gnostics of the early Christian centuries found themselves in this same awkward position. The more enlightened they became through spiritual experience, the less acceptable they were to the mainstream priests of the fledgling Christian faith. The Way of inspiration and visionary experience of the Divine was denounced by the orthodox, following the tradition of Irenaeus (d. 202) and Tertullian (d. 220), who wrote polemic treatises castigating gnostic teachings. Eventually the waters of the Spirit that had irrigated the emerging Christian movement were confined to specific, authorized channels, and the doctrines of the Church became concretized as Peter's Rock—the monolithic institutional Church formed on the hierarchical model of the Roman Empire, whose patriarchs guard the walls and whose cardinals take a solemn oath to prevent scandal and keep secret anything that might cause harm to the Holy Roman Catholic Church. Like hierarchical priesthoods of ancient Israel, "The shepherds have been shepherding themselves instead of the sheep" (Ezekiel 34).

What began as a movement springing from the life, ministry, and teachings of the Jewish rabbi Yeshua, the Nazorean, celebrated in small gatherings around a Eucharistic meal of bread and fish, became a centralized liturgical religion promulgated by a hierarchy of exclusively male—often celibate—priests. At the same time, in the late second century and thereafter, the voice of his beloved, symbolic of his community, was silenced, a condition solidified by the orthodox when the First Epistle of Timothy was accepted as an authentic teaching of Saint Paul: "I do not allow women to teach or to have authority over men." Based on linguistic studies comparing 1 Timothy with letters confirmed as written by Paul, modern scholars recognize that this letter to Timothy cannot be attributed to Paul. But that determination comes sixteen hundred years too late to restore the voices of women to Western civilization—women who, like the bride herself, had been forced into figurative exile. By the fourth century, the voices of female leaders of the Church, whose early ministry was modeled on that of Mary Magdalene—and on the sister-wives of apostles and brothers of Jesus traveling as missionary partners in his entourage—were largely silenced and are only now being recovered.

And what exactly are we intent on recovering? The gnostic gospels provide us with clear testimony about the status of Mary Magdalene as an apostle in her own right. The Book of Acts, Paul's Epistles, and other writings of early Church fathers testify that women originally had important leadership roles in established Christian communities—deaconesses and presbyters. In his polemic against gnostics, Tertullian expresses dismay that their communities allow women to perform baptisms and exorcisms. With Mary Magdalene as their role model, the claim of women to equality with their male counterparts in the institution is unquestionably justified. This view of Magdalene establishes that, at the very least, she was the female counterpart of Peter, who, lest we forget, denied Jesus three times on the night of his master's arrest and distinguished himself further by his absence at both cross and tomb.

Many contemporary Christians argue that restoring women to leadership roles in their communities would redress the imbalance inherent in Christianity by reestablishing the powerful model of gender equality and shared authority indigenous to the original Christian experience. Irrefutable historical justification exists for this movement. Already in recent decades, some mainstream churches have welcomed women into ministry where they share decision making with male priests and pastors, although several of the more conservative Christian denominations refuse to consider such a radical move, believing it to be unprecedented and nonscriptural. These denominations cling to the model of

PLATE 9: Joan Beth Clair, *Alive in Her: She Who Is Perfectly Empty and Perfectly Full.* Copyright © 2002 by Joan Beth Clair.

PLATE 10:
Giotti di Bondone (1266–1336), *Mary Magdalene's Voyage to Marseilles.* Magdalene Chapel, Lower Church, San Francesco, Assisi. Copyright © Elio Ciol/Corbis.

PLATE 11: "Exile Carpet" fragments (c. A.D. 150–180).
Photograph Courtesy of Jeremy Pine.

PLATE 12: Jacopo Robusti Tintoretto (1518–1594), *Christ in the House of Martha and Mary*. Alte Pinakothek, Munich. Courtesy of Scala/ Art Resource, NY.

PLATE 13: Segna di Buonaventure
(c. 1298–c. 1331), *Saint Magdalen*.
Alte Pinakothek, Munich.

PLATE 14: Robert
Campin (c. 1375–1444),
Saint Barbara. Museo
del Prado, Madrid.
Courtesy of Giraudon/
Art Resource, NY.

PLATE 16: Dante Gabriel Rossetti
(1828–1882), *Mary Magdalene*. Samuel
and Mary R. Bancroft Memorial,
Delaware Art Museum, Wilmington.

the twelve male apostles as the leaders exclusively designated by Christ to guide his Church. Yet, as we have discussed, clear scriptural evidence points to both male and female disciples following Jesus and to early Christian evangelists who traveled and gave witness to the good news as missionary couples. And always, Mary Magdalene—not a male apostle—was reported to be the first witness to the resurrection.

Restoring women to positions of leadership in Christian churches—allowing them to preach, to teach, and to prophesy, as in the earliest communities—is appropriate and necessary. Justice demands it.

But restoring this original model for shared power, position, and authority in institutional Christian denominations is not nearly enough. While it corrects the historical gender discrimination of hierarchical Christian institutions, a political move toward gender equality on the literal, historical plane will not heal the wasteland and cause the desert to bloom. Restoring Mary Magdalene as an apostle equal in status to Peter will not restore the lost bride of the ancient mythology of the sacred king.

We must be willing to heed the voice of the Holy One who says: "Behold, I am doing something new! . . . I am putting water in the desert and rivers in the wasteland for my chosen people to drink!" (Isaiah 43:19, 20).

It is time to celebrate the nuptials of the Lamb and to embrace his bride—the woman who from the very dawn of the Christian story represented the land and the assembly of believers, the Church. When we—at last!—embrace the sacred union that allows us to image the Divine as loving partners, streams of living water will flow from the throne of God "for the healing of the nations" (Revelation 21).

5

The Fragile Boat

There were three who walked with the Lord: Mary his
mother, and his mother's sister, and Miriam Magdalene,
known as his companion. For him, Miriam is a sister,
a mother, and a wife.

GOSPEL OF PHILIP[1]

The gospels do not state that Jesus was celibate. Nor do they state
that he was married. In the first century, in the culture to which Jesus
belonged, a man's marriage was virtually taken for granted. Indeed, had
Jesus been celibate, the fact would probably have been mentioned, as
it was for Simeon ben Azzai, a renowned second-century Jewish rabbi
who some scholars believe consecrated himself to God and remained
unmarried. But even in this often cited case, evidence is conflicting, for
elsewhere in the Talmud, Simeon is said to have married in his youth
a daughter of Rabbi Akiba and later divorced her, presumably remaining celibate thereafter, dedicating himself to his studies.[2] Five separate
Jewish sources mention the unique devotion of Rabbi Simeon to the
Torah, which he considered his bride, precisely because his lifestyle
was so unusual in the Judaism of his day. Theirs was a society where
marriage was the accepted norm; it was the duty of a father to find a
bride for his son soon after the boy reached puberty, and in any event
before the young man celebrated his twentieth birthday.[3] The unusual

status of Simeon was recorded precisely because it violated the norm. Yet nowhere in scripture does anyone say that Jesus was not married. The obligation to marry and to have children was taken seriously, especially among descendants of the Davidic bloodline, from whom the Messiah was expected to stem. Parents of this bloodline were likely to be conscientious in providing their son with a suitable wife. Paul's letter to Romans is the earliest attestation that Jesus was of David's seed: ". . . regarding his son, who as to his human nature was a descendant of David" (Romans 1:2).

Today's Bible scholars, in an effort to uphold the celibacy and absolute chastity of Jesus, sometimes cite two other possible examples of first-century celibacy among the Jews: the Essenes and the Therapeutae. Both appear to me to be far-fetched. These groups were isolated communities living in monasteries outside of mainstream Judaism, and there is no definitive proof that they were lifelong celibates. They may have become monks after fulfilling their traditional obligations of marriage and parenthood. Philo and Josephus both mention celibacy in connection with the Essenes, but absolute lifelong chastity of the Essenes cannot be confirmed, nor can their alleged celibacy. Graves of females and children were excavated at Qumran, to the surprise of archaeologists, who had expected only graves of male monastics at the commune's complex near the Dead Sea. More likely, temporary chastity was imposed during the time they spent in the community of Essenes. And possibly, they entered the community only after fathering children, which was demanded by Jewish law and custom. In any case, the Essenes were not mainstream Jews, but were regarded by their countrymen as radical antiestablishment outsiders. The other group whose celibacy is cited, the Therapeutae, did not live in Judaea at all. They welcomed initiates of both sexes at the monastery they occupied on the shores of a lake in Egypt, far from Jewish mainstream society, which was subject to the Torah and the teachings of Rabbinical Judaism.

While the anomalies we mention existed in Jesus' time, the norm in Judaism was marriage. Their language had no word for *bachelor*— the word used in modern Hebrew is *ravak,* which means "empty."[4]

Celibacy was not a desirable state: "It is not good for the man to be alone. I will make him a partner like himself" (Genesis 2:18). That was God speaking. But wives were not awarded special attention or status, and in most cases where they are mentioned, they are nameless. In the gospel, we are inadvertently told that Peter was married, but the name of his wife is not mentioned. Jesus heals Peter's mother-in-law (also nameless!) who is in bed with a fever (Matthew 8:14). And we know from Paul's first epistle to the church at Corinth that the other apostles and brothers of Jesus were also married and traveled with their wives (1 Corinthians 9:5), but these women, too, remain anonymous.

In an earlier chapter, we examined the scriptural basis for identifying the bride of Jesus. Based on what we know of ancient rites of the sacrificed king, his wife had to be the woman who was later reunited with him at the tomb. The conflation of the woman who anointed Jesus with Mary Magdalene was immediate in the minds of those who heard the gospels because pagan citizens of the Roman Empire recognized these roles of the bride in familiar rites from fertility cults indigenous to their lands. Combining Mary Magdalene and the sister of Lazarus into one person is also taken for granted in the third-century gnostic treatise Pistis Sophia, where the women named among the disciples of Jesus gathered to hear his teachings are the mother of Jesus, Mary (Magdalene), Martha, and Salome. Here Mary is assumed to be the one called the Magdalene although her honorific is not stated in this treatise or in any other gnostic text except the Gospel of Philip. To the author of the Pistis Sophia, logic or perhaps tradition apparently suggests that Martha, universally perceived to be the sister of Mary Magdalene, should be added to the customary list of three women known to have traveled with Jesus during his ministry—the three ointment bearers explicitly named in Mark 16:1. Is there any doubt that the Mary mentioned in the Pistis Sophia is the sister of Martha from Bethany (Luke 10; John 11 and 12), the one who had "chosen the better part" and enjoyed a reputation as the most faithful follower of Jesus?

The Sacred King

Following the resurrection, danger to the royal bloodline of the acclaimed Davidic Messiah would have been reason enough to hide his wife and any children of their union. To taunt the crowd that gathered to watch the execution of Jesus at Golgotha, the Roman centurion posted a scroll on the cross above the head of the Jewish hero. Abbreviated INRI, the epithet read "Jesus the Nazorean, King of the Jews" (John 19:19) or, as in the synoptic gospels, "Jesus, King of the Jews." The issue was obviously his acclaimed kingship. It was not the Jews who crucified Jesus; the Romans crucified Jesus for inciting insurrection, subjecting him to a punishment reserved for rebels and slaves.

On the morning of the third day after the Crucifixion, Roman authorities were faced with a volatile situation in the crowded streets of Jerusalem. Instead of a dead insurrectionist whose brutal execution had been designed to intimidate future rebels so unwise as to challenge Rome, the procurator Pontius Pilate and his political allies were confronted with the Easter proclamation, accosted by rumors of the resurrection of the crucified king of the Jews. Like familiar god-kings of neighboring cults ritually sacrificed at the vernal equinox, Jesus was alive, raised from the dead! He had been seen by many of his followers and was suddenly elevated to the status of Tammuz, Dionysus, and Osiris, pagan gods who had survived the grave in their own myths and liturgies. The crucified Jewish rabbi Yeshua—proclaimed the Son of David by palm-waving enthusiasts in the streets of Jerusalem and followed by grieving women of Jerusalem who bewailed him during the procession to Golgotha (Luke 23:27)— was now seen to embody the mythology of the sacrificed bride-groom/king ubiquitous in religions of the ancient Near East. The prophet Ezekiel mentions the women of Jerusalem "mourning for Tammuz" (Ezekiel 8:14), so the scenario was not new in Israel; it was ancient. The news of the resurrection spread spontaneously among Jewish pilgrims thronging Jerusalem for the feast of Passover.

Several high-profile critics of this interpretation of the Passion narrative drawn from the myth of the sacred king assert that they cannot imagine early Christians, many of them of Jewish background, including pagan rites or mythology in their sacred texts. Their position, if not disingenuous, is naïve. The mythology of the sacrificed king is already there—in plain sight—in the Passion narrative found in the final chapters of the four accepted gospels. How can Christians ignore it? How can they explain it away? The Church fathers were well aware that the gospels contained parallels to pagan rites and myths and deplored the association, with some suggesting that the pagans must have copied Christ rather than admit that the pagan rites were antecedents of the Christian myths. Have modern apologists forgotten that the gospels were written not in Hebrew or Aramaic for Jewish converts, but in Greek for the converts of the pagan Roman Empire? Of course, these pagans would have recognized in Christ the mythology and rites of the sacred bridegroom king, sacrificed for his people. Throughout the New Testament he is identified with the Bridegroom. How could they have failed to recognize in Mary Magdalene his archetypal bride?

At that moment in history, the original Easter morning, danger posed by Roman authorities to the wife of Jesus and any children of their union would have been acute. And at exactly that moment in the historical record, the written trail goes cold; Mary Magdalene and the siblings from Bethany are notably absent in the Acts of the Apostles attributed to Luke and in the epistles of Paul. The friends of Jesus appear to have recognized the danger and taken steps to hide his family from anyone who wished them ill. Their perception was based on a clear and present danger; the Romans hunted down blood relatives of Jesus for several generations thereafter, apparently executing them in many cases. The priests in Jerusalem are accused of executing James the Just (the younger brother of Jesus?) in about A.D. 62, either by stoning or by throwing him off the Temple wall or, according to Hegesippus, both. The *desposynoi*, those related to Jesus by blood kinship, remained leaders of the community for a generation, then gradually faded into oblivion, surfacing later in the legends and lore of Celtic churches.

The whereabouts of the wife of Jesus would have been a carefully guarded secret for at least a generation, until after the death of Paul, whom the family of Jesus and the Jerusalem Christians had no reason to trust. This concern for her safety would have been even more intense if she were expecting a child at the time of the Crucifixion. Only after Paul's death were the gospels containing stories of Jesus' life and ministry committed to writing. And even then, especially in the earlier gospels, the identity of his wife is veiled rather than explicit. Finally the author of the fourth and latest gospel (written in 90–95) feels free to identify the woman who anoints Jesus as the sister of Lazarus of Bethany. Perhaps enough time had elapsed that the author feels safe identifying the woman thus cast in the role of royal bride.

The Book of Acts tells the story of the eleven apostles and the miracle of Pentecost, but no mention is made of Mary Magdalene, Martha, or Lazarus. In spite of their prominence in the four gospels, the siblings have vanished from the community of disciples gathered in the upper room in Jerusalem in Luke's account of Christian origins. Because Luke is reported to have been a close associate of Paul, logic suggests that he would not have been privy to closely guarded family secrets. This may explain also why Luke alone places the anointing scene—so reminiscent of ancient nuptial rites of hieros gamos proclaiming the kingship of the bridegroom—in a remote village in faraway Galilee, as far as possible from the Mount of Olives and the home of the three youthful siblings whom Jesus loved. Luke alone of all the gospel writers does not call Jesus' favored companion Maria h Magdalhnh. He introduces her by calling her "the woman called Magdalene," which seems to imply that her name is an epithet or title rather than the name of her hometown (8:1) and at the tomb he calls her "h Magdalhnh Maria" (24:10). I think it is conceivable that by calling her a sinner and distorting her epithet, Luke was deliberately downgrading the powerful story of Jesus' anointing by the woman at the banquet. In effect, he stole her voice for two millennia.

The Bark of Mary

When the historical trail is obscured in mists of time, legend takes over. While the Roman Catholic Church is often called the Bark of Peter, there was another boat in the earliest Christian traditions—the Bark of Mary, custodian of the gnostic tradition, the Way of the heart. A legend emerged in Ephesus in the fifth century telling that the Apostle John brought the Virgin Mary and Mary Magdalene to that city—once sacred to the goddess Artemis—and that both women died there. But in direct contrast to this tale, another surprisingly credible story survives on the coast of France. The French legend claims that the Mary called the Magdalene fled the tyranny of Roman occupation in Palestine and sought refuge on the shores of the Mediterranean in the Roman province of Gaul. The fourth-century version of the story alleges that Mary Magdalene preached the gospel in Marseilles.[5] Later legends embellished the story: The entire family from Bethany, along with their friends, had been forced into exile, traveling in a boat with no oars or rudder, cast adrift on the Mediterranean Sea, and somehow, by the grace of God, landing safely at a place called Ratis on the coast of Gaul, in A.D. 42 or thereabouts. At that time, Ratis was an offshore island in whose temple Cybele, the Great Goddess, in her manifestation as Rhea, Artemis, and Isis, had been worshipped for hundreds of years.[6]

On the wall of the Holy Sepulcher in Jerusalem is a drawing of a small boat and the inscription "We went." Could it be an ancient fossil of the legend of the family members present at the entombment of Jesus who are said to have made the voyage to Gaul? These Christian refugees fleeing persecution in their homeland are credited as the first witnesses to Christ on French soil, and their legend maintains that they brought with them the Holy Grail. The story was sown in the fertile fields of Provence, in southern France, where the cult of Mary Magdalene flourished over the centuries, where numerous old stone churches bear her name, and where she is the ubiquitous patroness of springs and vineyards, perfume makers and apothecaries.

The legend of the émigré Christians is told and retold, published in about 1267 in the *Legenda Aurea* (Golden Legend) of Jacobus de Voragine, a Dominican priest and later archbishop of Genoa, who names the entire party on the boat, including Marcella, the maidservant of Martha. Other legends mention a servant named Sarah, a name that in Hebrew means "princess." The child is characterized as preadolescent— between nine and twelve years of age—and is called Sarah the Egyptian in medieval lore. Subsequently, this legend forms the basis for the widespread belief that a child of Mary and Jesus survived the Crucifixion and was brought to Gaul.[7]

Details about the refugee family in exile are sparse. The passengers on the fragile bark, the Bark of Mary, included Lazarus, Martha, Mary Jacobi (mother of James), and Mary Salome, the latter two whom we encountered earlier as ointment bearers in Mark's gospel—the women who accompanied Mary Magdalene to the tomb on Easter morning. The *Legenda Aurea* of Jacobus de Voragine mentions two other male companions as well, Maximin and blind Cedony, traveling with the Bethany family and their maidservant. The idea that the boat had no oars or rudder was a symbolic way of saying that it was at the mercy of God and dependent on the guidance of the Holy Spirit, like the bark of our own souls on the sea of life.

Somehow this story of the precarious journey later became conflated with the legend of Joseph of Arimathea, who is said to have brought the Holy Grail to Western Europe, where the story incubates undisturbed for centuries, making its way into art, artifact, and folklore. Several medieval paintings show Joseph holding a chalice under the cross to catch the blood streaming from the side of the dying Savior, literal pictorial support of the myth that the Grail contained the royal and holy blood of Jesus. A related legend maintains that Joseph of Arimathea brought two cruets containing the blood and sweat of Jesus to Glastonbury, in addition to a hawthorn staff that bloomed when he planted it in English soil.

I am now going to make a radical, but, in light of the combination of facts and legends that we have encountered, I believe quite sensible speculation. Suppose Jesus was married in his youth, as dictated by the Torah and rabbis of Judaism in the first century, and that, after the birth of several children, his wife tragically died. At that point, having fulfilled the law to beget heirs, Jesus would have no requirement to remarry. He would have fulfilled the commandment of the Torah, so the Pharisees would have had no grounds for criticizing him on this issue, but he would have had no wife during the hypothetical intervening years. He eventually embarked on his ministry, traveled to

Jerusalem several times, and encountered the wealthy family at Bethany, who were apparently devoted to him. Finding her irresistible, he formed a dynastically suitable marriage alliance with Mary, the younger sister of this family. We don't know exactly when, or how, but rumors of their intimacy survive in the gospels and apocrypha, so we speculate that it was so. If she was pregnant at the time of his crucifixion, she would have been placed immediately under the protection of his most trustworthy friends—not the apostles who were hiding somewhere in Jerusalem, but those most devoted friends who remained with her at the cross: Joseph of Arimathea and Nicodemus. Speculation suggests that the siblings of Bethany may have been the children of Nicodemus himself, who, according to the Jewish Talmud, was a man of notable wealth in Jerusalem. If the wedding was the dynastic joining of the Shoot, or royal heir, of the Davidic line of Judah, with a dynastic heiress of Benjamin, it might well have been kept quiet out of fear of Roman intervention and eventually written out of the story altogether, except for the fossils left almost accidentally in the gospel narratives: the messianic anointing of the king and the reunion in the garden, two events that identify the Christ couple of ancient mythology. To me, this hypothetical scenario makes sense because it explains how Jesus could have been married to Mary, the sister of Lazarus, and at the same time why some later Christians believed a tradition that he was celibate.

According to legends indigenous to France, Mary Magdalene traveled south to Marseilles with Maximin and preached the gospel there before retiring to seclusion at Sainte Baume, a cave formerly involved in worship of the fertility goddess, where Mary is said to have remained a hermit for thirty years, until her death. Wonderful frescoes on church walls in northern Italy portray the story of Mary Magdalene, often in panels that show scenes from her life: the raising of her brother Lazarus, the anointing of Jesus at the banquet, the arrival on the coast of France with her family and friends (plate 10).

The French legend maintains that the other two Marys remained in the little coastal town in the Camargue that now bears their names: Les Saintes Maries de la Mer, Saint Marys by the Sea. Their youthful maidservant Sarah stayed with them, according to the legend, and all three are honored every May 23–25 in a colorful folk festival that celebrates the arrival of these earliest Christians bringing the good news to the shores of Europe twenty-five years before the first gospel was written. Lazarus is said to have traveled on to Marseilles, eventually becoming a bishop, and Martha to Tarascon, where local folklore holds that she killed a dragon.

While French traditions declare that the apostle Philip evangelized Gaul, it seems more plausible that the text of the gnostic gospel attributed to Philip, with its assertions about the three Marys who accompanied Jesus and his intimate relationship with Mary Magdalene, somehow made the voyage across the sea from Egypt to Provence, carrying the seeds of the Grail legend that flourished there.

The Exile Carpet

A recently discovered artifact may, if authentic, throw even more light on this legend, placing its origin a thousand years earlier than the medieval version of the story widespread in Europe since the thirteenth century. In 2004, a man contacted me by e-mail with an amazing story to tell. Jeremy Pine, an American dealer in antique textiles and artifacts, was living abroad and traveling widely in central Asia, treasure hunting in connection with his antiquities business. Almost a decade ago, Pine was shown fragments of a severely damaged pile carpet that appeared worthless except for its obvious antiquity. The original carpet would have measured about twenty-eight inches by forty-eight inches and was apparently of early Christian origin. Several of the people depicted in the rug were surrounded by halos. Intrigued by the images, Pine submitted a sample from the fragments to the Rafter Radiocarbon Laboratory in New Zealand for carbon-14 dating analysis, and was astonished at the test results: The carpet was dated in two separate tests to a period in the mid-second century, A.D. 150–180, making it one of the oldest Christian artifacts in existence.

Because they are organic, textiles are vulnerable to heat, moisture, and vermin, so the fact that fragments of a prayer rug from this early Christian era survived at all is remarkable in itself. Pine's theory is that the carpet's original Egyptian/gnostic owners may have fled east from persecutions in or near Alexandria, eventually making their way to the Himalayan foothills, where the cool dry air effectively kept the precious carpet in cold storage for more than fifteen hundred years. In its way, the amazing discovery of these rug remnants could be similar to chance discoveries of the sacred texts at the Qumran and Nag Hammadi sites. The designer of the possibly second-century prayer rug appears to have known the legend of the holy family of Jesus who fled from Palestine as refugees in a little boat. The surviving fragments of the oval-shaped carpet show that the original piece was divided into seven sections containing pictures of people traveling in little boats with no sails or rudders (plate 11).

We can see that the two upper figures, one twice as large as the other, have red-gold hair and are riding in little blue boats surrounded by golden halos. The dark-haired figures in the two lower sections have baggage in their boats, suggesting that they are carrying their belongings, and they have no halos. Jeremy Pine surmises that the central figure, larger than the others and surrounded by a double halo and four lion masks, may represent Christ himself, the Lion of Judah, confirmed by the X motif of the carpet's sections, because the Greek letter X—*chi*—is the early Christian symbol for Christos. Further proof of the Christian context of the motif in the carpet is the mark on the forehead of the little figure in each boat. It is most likely the sign of the cross—the monogram of Christ—that traditionally marked adherents of some early Christian sects as servants of the Lord: "[A]nd his servants shall serve him. And they shall see his face, and his name shall be on their foreheads" (Revelation 22: 3b–4).

An experienced dealer in antique textiles for more than thirty years, Jeremy Pine believes that this carpet was woven in Alexandria, a cosmopolitan city known as the early home of certain Christian gnostics, some of whom honored images of their favorite sages and teachers and claimed that Mary Magdalene, Martha, and Salome were the direct source of their beliefs. In his polemic *Contra Celsus,* Origen quoted a passage from the pagan Celsus (written around A.D. 170) regarding Christian sects who followed teachings of women disciples of Jesus.

Fig. 5.1. This is a drawing of the Exile Carpet as it might have looked had it not been damaged by folding. See also plate 11.

Describing the prayer rug as pre-Coptic, Jeremy Pine notes its primitive, almost cartoonlike figures and the similarity of their crescent-shaped boats with the shell of a first-century fishing boat discovered during excavations several years ago buried in the sandy beach of the Sea of Galilee. In the opinion of the custodian of this unusual artifact, every detail known about the carpet fragments is consistent with the Grail legend, the "great secret of the Middle Ages"—that the persecuted and exiled family of Jesus sailed away in a tiny boat. Jeremy Pine asserts the rug may have been created by Christians who believed that the surviving child of Jesus and Mary Magdalene was a daughter. The designer of the carpet depicted a much smaller replica of the blond mother, possibly the Magdalene so often portrayed with strawberry blond hair in later artworks. Perhaps Mary really had reddish blond hair. In the ancient world, red hair was very rare and seems to have had a certain stigma attached to it: Redheads were often ostracized, for their hair color apparently carried connotations of demonic possession, which, in addition to her passionate nature, may be another reason it was so often attributed to Mary. Alternatively, her red hair may have instigated the rumor of her possession by demons, the malaise alleged in Luke 8:2. Perhaps her red hair, with its suggested attributes of tempera-ment and passion, are what made her so irresistible.

A surprising feature of the rug remnant is the blue boats in which the two figures, presumed to be a mother and daughter, are riding. Why are the boats blue? A replica of the boat in which the three Marys arrived at the present site of Saintes Maries de la Mer is displayed in the basilica there—the Church of Our Lady by the Sea—and it, too, is painted bright blue. In addition, several fourteenth-century frescoes depicting scenes of Mary Magdalene and her friends also include a blue boat. Murals painted by Giovanni (c. 1365) at the San Croce Basilica in Florence are similar to the Magdalene panels painted by Giotto (c. 1320) on the walls in the crypt of the Church of Saint Francis in Assisi (see plate 10). Among the ancients, blue—the color of the sky, the heavenly abode of the gods and goddesses—was associated with divinity, while purple was symbolic of royalty, expressing a mingling of the crimson associated with flesh and the blue of divinity. The term *blue-blooded* referring to noble lineage takes on a new dimension.

Another surprising enigma in the prayer carpet is a pair of blue ducks shown near the boat in the bottom-right-hand section, serving to verify that the background is indeed water. At the same time, the ducks may have an important function as a symbolic reference to Osiris and Isis, the god-goddess couple of Egyptian mythology. In the liturgical chants from *The Burden of Isis,* mentioned in chapter 3, we find a line that refers to the goddess Isis as a duck: Speaking to her brother/husband

Osiris, Isis calls herself "thy duck, thy sister Isis."[8] Because the mythology of Isis and Osiris—the sacred marriage, separation, and eventual reunion of the divine couple—is so similar to the mythology of Jesus and Mary Magdalene, the ducks might be interpreted as a symbolic link between the Christian couple portrayed in the carpet and their royal Egyptian predecessors. Admittedly, this interpretation of the carpet fragments is speculative, but the carpet is very real. It needs to be examined and discussed by scholars and experts from several disciplines who can sort out its origin, history, and probable meaning. But at this early date in its reemergence from an obscure hiding place, it has intriguing possibilities that appear to have connections to the Great Heresy. It could indeed have been a cherished relic of refugee Christians who fled to Kashmir or India when they were forced out of their homes in Israel or Egypt.

Early Christians did not worship in churches. Often they gathered in people's homes to share their faith and celebrate a Eucharistic meal. They may have created the carpet picturing a central tenet of their beliefs and perhaps carried it to their meetings, unfolding it on a table or on the floor and gathering around it for their shared meal or prayer service. If these textile fragments are from that era, as the carbon dating indicates, they may portray an important belief of their community, which may well have been the belief that the wife and child of Jesus survived, later to become the foundation for the heresy of the Sangraal. While suggestions found in the pictures in the rug might be explained by other myths and interpretations, the Grail story incorporates them with no apparent inconsistencies. As the fragments of this carpet are submitted to the scrutiny of museum curators and other scholars of antique treasures, we will learn more about the story shown in its pile fibers. The most amazing thing is not that early Christians created such an artifact, but that it has survived to tell its story.

Sarah the Egyptian

In recent years, much has been made of the artifact known as the Holy Grail. People searching for ancient drinking cups and chalices have diligently combed through art and lore for traces of the vessel that once contained the blood of Christ. Of course, there must have been an actual cup from which Jesus drank at the Passover meal he shared with his friends. But is that drinking cup really the Holy Grail of myth and legend? Numerous views circulate about the origins of the legends, but I believe the most probable theory, the one that fits best into the relevant parameters, is the suggestion that the Sangraal was not really an artifact at all, but was a symbolic reference to the bloodline itself—the blood royal *(sang raal)* of the Davidic kings of Israel.[9] The relevant term is *royal*. Royal bloodlines are not carried around in a jar. The vessel of the royal bloodline, the sacred container, would have been Mary Magdalene herself, extended to any child born of her union with Jesus, but especially to a daughter, because a cup or chalice bears distinctly feminine symbolism.

The child who survives in the French versions of the legend can be only the child on the boat, little Saint Sarah, said to be the serving girl of the two Marys from across the sea, although her name means "princess" in her native tongue. The face of her effigy, housed in the crypt of the Basilica of Our Lady of the Sea in the village of Les Saintes Maries de la Mer, is black as ebony, possibly a symbolic blackness reminiscent of the bride in the Song of Songs, "swarthy from her labor in her brothers' vineyards." Could Sarah be the daughter of the "dark" bride of the Christian myth? This darkness could be a symbolic reference to the hidden and scorned status of the royal Davidic bloodline of the princes of Judah now in exile, whose faces were once white as milk but are now black as soot: They are "unrecognized in the streets" (Lamentations 4:7–8). The standard interpretation is that Sarah was black because she was Egyptian, but the dark countenance of the child could as easily point to her status as a refugee in exile—lost to history and to consciousness. The sun-darkened maidservant is subsequently called Sarah the Egyptian in European folklore.

Like Cinderella, another sooty-faced princess from a faraway land, Sarah is obscure, unrecognized, and relegated to the status of a servant to her relatives. She may, in fact, have been the prototype for the Cinderella story, which surfaces as early as the ninth century in

Western Europe.[10] Every year, at the folk festival in Les Saintes Maries de la Mer, Roma (Gypsies) of the region dress little Sarah's statue in layers of many-colored silk and organza robes fashioned by Roma seamstresses of various tribes. The extravagant dresses are reminiscent of Cinderella's exquisite ball gown, another poignant connection with the sooty-faced princess of European fairy tale. Roma men in full native regalia, mounted on snow white horses of the Camargue, form an escort that accompanies the statue of Saint Sarah in a procession through the streets of the village and out to the sea. Their horses stamping in the ocean waves, moving forward as the tide comes in, the Roma hold the statue aloft while several thousand pilgrims sing hymns blessing Saint Sarah, celebrating her arrival on the shores of Gaul: "Vive Sainte Sarah!"

Meanwhile, appalled by the throng of foreign visitors flocking to this quasi-religious folk celebration, local French clergy downplay the festival, reminding the faithful that Saint Sarah is not mentioned anywhere in Christian scripture. She is a legend, they insist, speaking to a standing-room-only crowd of devotees assembled for Mass on her feast day, May 24, in the Basilica of Our Lady of the Sea. Apparently the local Roman Catholic bishop would prefer that this child saint continue in relative obscurity and exile, along with her royal mother, the Magdalene, whose story has been distorted almost beyond retrieval by those who called her a prostitute.

There is no birth certificate for Sarah, no genealogies that irrefutably confirm her origins, nothing that constitutes proof of her existence or identity in the left-brained world of academics. However, legends often contain kernels of truth too dangerous to be asserted as fact but nonetheless significant. Oral traditions are often more reliable than history, which is known to record the bias of the writer. What kernel of truth lies behind the story of Saint Sarah? Her relevance does not lie in the claims of later peers of Europe to exalted status by virtue of their blue-blooded lineage, but rather, she serves as proof of the sacred marriage—the union of the archetypal bride and bridegroom—at the heart of the Christian story. Her existence in legend provides strong evidence that belief in the sacred union of Christ and Mary Magdalene was celebrated at all levels—physical as well as emotional and spiritual—and that the memory of this union was widely dispersed—even after its deliberate suppression—by means of an underground stream of esoteric teachings. The research of the folklorist Kathleen McGowan, recently published in her book *The Expected One,* confirms that stories of Mary Magdalene and the bloodline of Jesus survive in an underground reservoir of folk memories in the Languedoc—in spite of dungeon, fire, and sword wielded by the Inquisition in an attempt to wipe them out.

The carpet fragments from the second century, as interpreted by Jeremy Pine, suggest that someone in the second or third century knew and believed that story as well. This was the "greatest story never told"—the story of Christ's full humanity, lived in intimate relationship with his wife. Despite attempts to blot out all memory of this belief of the earliest Christians, it survived in art, in artifact, and in the folk- and fairy tales of Western civilization.[11]

The Merovingian Fish

The *Golden Legend* of Blessed Jacobus de Voragine, with its embellished stories of Mary Magdalene, was published in Italy in 1267. About a decade later, the tomb containing bones of Mary Magdalene was discovered in the crypt of the church in Saint Maximin, a Gallo-Roman town renamed in honor of her refugee compatriot who became its first bishop. Meanwhile, at about the same time but several hundred miles away, in the town of Metz in Alsace-Lorraine, an unknown artist painted a strange picture on oak planks that formed the wall of a building (fig. 5.2).

The double-tailed mermaid was here linked to the Great Fish, the ubiquitous symbol for Christ, whose epithet Jesus Christ, Son of God, Savior provided the acronym Ιχθυς—the Greek word for "fish"—a symbol by which he is still widely recognized. In the heyday of the royal Merovingian Franks, Metz was their seat of power, and legends of their ancestor Merovée included a preposterous tale that his birth had resulted from his mother's liaison with a marine monster—half man, half fish.

Other fishy legends and stories linked this Frankish royal family to the mermaid as well, and her image occurs frequently among medieval watermarks (dated between 1280 and 1600).[12] Who is this mermaid, the ancestress of the Merovingians? Who but the diminutive of the Great Goddess relegated to the depths of our consciousness, deep-sixed to the bottom of the sea! The tempera-on-wood portraits of the mermaid and the fish appear to be symbolic renderings of the fishes—the lord and lady of the astrological Age of Pisces. Christ was recognized as the Fish—avatar of the age to come—from the dawn of the Christian story. It was his spouse—the second fish in the zodiac sign, which resembles the yin/yang symbol—who was denied, scorned, and vilified, who was sent into exile and unrecognized in the streets. Mermaid watermarks frequently have *M*s in their fins and often in their crowns, attesting to their royal status. Often they have fleurs-de-lis as well, the symbol associated with the French royal lineage. An early example is carved in stone, probably from the sixth century, again in the town of Metz, the ancestral home of the Merovingians. The double-tailed mermaid is surrounded by a vine with numerous fleurs-de-lis budding along its stems.[13] Because in the Hebrew scriptures the vine of Judah is called the Lord's cherished plant (Isaiah 5:7), the vine motif has powerful associations with the alleged surviving bloodline linked to the royal lineage of the Lion of Judah, Christ himself. Apparently the legend of

Fig. 5.2. The Lord and Lady of the Fishes (thirteenth century, Metz)

the sacred marriage was not confined to the Mediterranean coastal regions of northern Italy and Provence, but inspired artifacts as far as the northern reaches of Roman hegemony in Europe—and beyond.

The heresy of the royal Davidic bloodline and its European heirs survived in several other media, including the written word. In fact, much of the art and lore of medieval Europe can be read as a midrash, or interpretation of Hebrew Bible references, to promises made to the heirs of the Davidic bloodline. European history can be read in this light. The German poet Wolfram von Eschenbach claimed that the Order of the Knights of the Temple of Solomon, known as the Knights Templar, were guardians of the Grail family. Wolfram is not explicit as to who or what the Grail family is, but he uses a provocative term for the Grail itself. He calls it the *lapsit exillis,* a Latinized phrase that can be translated as the "jewel" or "stone" in exile. Could he have been referring to the *other* rock—tenets held by adherents of the alternative Christian Church of Amor, in contrast to that of Roma, Peter's Rock, a common metaphor for the Roman Catholic Church? Perhaps Wolfram recognized the tenets of the Grail heresy, and the family itself, as a jewel in exile. This lost or hidden jewel—the family of the Grail with its great secret—was like the pearl of great price hidden in a field, a metaphor used by Jesus for the kingdom or reign of God.

The lost Grail, characterized in poetry and legend as the vessel that once contained the blood of Christ, has strong symbolic associations with Wolfram's elusive lapsit/jewel in exile. The wounded Fisher King will be healed of his thigh wound, the legend promises, and his kingdom, now a desolate wasteland, will be restored. This promise is consistent with the underlying theology of the sacred marriage: When the bride (the lost vessel) and bridegroom are happily reunited in the hieros gamos union, the entire domain rejoices and the joy and blessing from the bridal chamber spread out into the crops and herds, making them fertile. The lapsit exillis, like the elusive pearl of great price, is hidden or misunderstood; the object of the heroic quest is to restore it to consciousness. In Wolfram's poem, the bumpkin Parzifal—the archetypal fool or simpleton—pursues the quest and eventually accomplishes the mission. At the time Wolfram's poem was written, early in the thirteenth century, the great secret hidden for so long in Western traditions seemed poised to come forth into consciousness. But hope for the healing of the kingdom was short-lived, the dream aborted, the promise brutally suppressed by the Inquisition.

The Heretical Secret

In 1239, the flowering of the Grail legends was nipped in the bud by the formation of the Inquisition. The southern provinces of France were engulfed in a brutal genocide called the Albigensian Crusade (1209–1250), during which mercenary armies of the pope and French king collaborated to wipe out whole cities. The annals of the Inquisition do not make clear what the Cathars believed that the Roman Church found so unacceptable, but strong evidence asserts that one of their tenets of faith was the marriage union of Jesus and Mary Magdalene. In 1209, the French soldiers of Simon de Montfort swept into the walled town of Béziers and killed twenty thousand citizens, of whom many were Cathars. Some sought sanctuary in the church, and perished en masse when the building was torched.

This brutality is mentioned in a contemporaneous document describing the massacre at Béziers believed recorded by Pierre des Vaux-de-Cernay, a Cistercian monk writing in 1213 about the Albigensian Crusade and the campaign led by Simon de Montfort. Noting that the slaughter of the men, women, and children at Béziers had been accomplished by order of Pope Innocent III on July 22, the feast day of Mary Magdalene, the zealous monk declared that it was a "supreme justice of Providence" because the heretics claimed that Saint Mary Magdalene was the concubine of Jesus Christ.[14] In a second account by the same author, *A Description of the Cathars and Waldenses*, Pierre des Vaux-de-Cernay asserted that the heretics affirmed the marriage of Christ to Mary Magdalene. For this view, he may have relied in part on an earlier source found in *An Exposure of the Albigensian Heresies*, attributed to Ermengaud of Béziers, who supports the claim that "Cathars taught in their secret meetings that Mary Magdalene was the wife of Jesus Christ."[15] This thirteenth-century text asserts further that the Cathars taught that

Mary Magdalene was the Samaritan woman at the well and that they identified her also with the woman taken in adultery whom Christ exonerated. These spurious slanders of Mary Magdalene, ostensibly derived from Cathar doctrine, survived in a vastly distorted version well into the Reformation period, and were apparently believed by Martin Luther himself, who is quoted as saying that Jesus had sexual affairs with all three women.[16] The belief that Jesus and Mary Magdalene were beloveds was a widespread tenet for which the heretics of the Languedoc were brutally assaulted and slaughtered in the merciless Albigensian Crusade.

The bloody campaign against the Cathars culminated in 1244 with the fall of Montségur and the death by burning of the heretics who surrendered there. The Inquisition continued its hegemony in Europe for centuries thereafter. Still, the great heresy surfaced in art and artifact—in watermarks, paintings, tapestries—and in fairy tale and folklore. Tenets of the alternative church are illustrated in the trumps of the earliest tarot decks, which provide a flashcard catechism for the Grail heresy. These and various other vehicles for keeping the Great Secret alive are more thoroughly discussed in *The Woman with the Alabaster Jar,* but several other artworks are included among the illustrations in this volume to further demonstrate the point that certain artists knew and continued to perpetuate the secret tradition.

The Great Secret in Art

A famous painting by Tintoretto (plate 12) is *Christ in the House of Martha and Mary,* illustrating the text from Luke 10:38–42. Created about 1470–75, the painting contains numerous allusions to the secret union of Jesus and Mary of Bethany. Mary is seated at Jesus' feet and Martha complains because she needs help preparing the meal (Luke 10:39–40). In this painting, Mary's blue gown and red stole are the exact equal and opposite of the garments worn by Jesus. Their juxtaposition reminds us of the alchemist's woodcut of the king and queen representing masculine and feminine principles, crossing from left to right, right to left, illustrating the concept of the symbiotic union of left and right, male and female (see fig. 7.2, page 145).

In Tintoretto's painting, Mary is seated in an odd position facing Jesus. The odd posture is similar to that of a woman sitting on a birthing stool, and her right hand is cupped in an ancient symbolic invitation for sex. With his fingers, Jesus is apparently forming a vesica piscis, the archetypal symbol for the goddess of love and fertility, associated by gematria with Mary Magdalene herself![17] In the background, in the transom above the doorway, we find a grid of Xs, the most frequent symbol for the alternative medieval church—the Grail Church of Amor.[18] One esoteric symbol in a painting is not proof positive of its heretical meaning, but when the artist includes so many hints in a single scene, we have grounds to suspect he was making a deliberate statement. Because many medieval and Renaissance artists sipped from the waters of the "underground stream" of esoteric teachings, sharing their insights *sub rosa,* we should not be surprised to find a continuum of heretical symbols in their works, even—maybe especially!—in those based on texts from the gospels.

6

Desert Exile

And the woman fled into the wilderness where she
had a place prepared by God.

REVELATION 13:6

As we recall Mary Magdalene to our consciousness after the almost two millennia of desert exile, we should examine the important archetype she embodied during her long years of banishment, for in Christianity Mary Magdalene represents—par excellence—the feminine face of God and its incarnation in the female half of creation. So, too, she represents the painful separation of the beloveds, their quest for reunion, and their return to holy embrace. Celebrating Mary Magdalene as a faithful disciple, a most faithful follower or an apostle equal to Peter, even restoring her to an exalted position as companion of Jesus, falls short of restoring her as Sacred Partner and Archetypal Bride of the Eternal Bridegroom. To claim that the historical Mary Magdalene had a spiritual union with Jesus while denying her the status of spouse leaves her in the role of a dependent/subordinate friend of the Lord rather than his partner celebrated in the hieros gamos union at all levels of experience—similar to that manifested by numerous god and goddess couples of the ancient Near East.

Mary Magdalene does not stand alone, an isolated instance of the Goddess denied. Her story is a composite of stories and myths of numerous goddesses from the ancient world—goddesses of love, fertility, and wisdom. As the historical Mary Magdalene lived the archetypal pattern of sacred union with her beloved on the physical or literal plane, the mythological Magdalene incarnates the same pattern at a spiritual and metaphorical level. In examining the stories of various goddesses and heroines of ancient myths, we detect fundamental similarities with Mary Magdalene's story; and these stories, in turn, provide greater insights about the Magdalene.

The Myth of Orpheus

The Greek god that early Christians associated most closely with Jesus was Orpheus, the son of Apollo and Calliope, who was one of the Muses.[1] The music Orpheus played on his lyre was so sweet that it caused rocks to soften and tigers to shed tears. His melodies charmed all of creation and forced rivers to stop flowing. In due course, Orpheus fell in love with the beautiful Eurydice, and the two celebrated their nuptials. But soon thereafter, the shepherd Aristaeus was captivated by the beauty of the bride and lusted after her. When he made advances toward her, Eurydice fled from him, and in her haste stepped on a poisonous snake that bit her heel. She died and disappeared into Tartarus, the underworld domain of Pluto and Proserpine.

Distraught over the loss of his bride, Orpheus made his way to the throne room of the royal rulers of the underworld. Taking out his lyre, he composed a song acknowledging that all human beings ultimately belonged to the ruling couple of the realm of the dead, but begging them in their mercy to restore his beloved wife to him because she had suffered such a tragic and untimely death. Even the ghosts wept when he finished his song, and Pluto, touched by the suffering of the great lover-musician, gave him permission to redeem Eurydice. The ruler of the underworld allowed the young couple to leave Tartarus under one condition: Orpheus must lead his wife without looking back to see if she was following him. Eurydice walked with a limp, hindered by her injured heel, when the two lovers set out together to return to the land of the living, making their way along perilous dark and steep pathways.

Just before they reached the boundary between the world of the dead and of the living, Orpheus forgot Pluto's admonition and turned to ensure that Eurydice was still following him. In an instant she was borne away, stretching out her arms to him and calling out his name. All his impassioned pleas for a second chance to redeem her were rejected.

For the rest of his life, the bereaved Orpheus continued to make wonderful music but he spurned womankind, ignoring their advances and remaining celibate, ever faithful to the memory of the wife of his youth and mourning her untimely death. Finally, a group of Thracian maidens, angered at his rejection, set upon Orpheus, killed him, and savagely rent his corpse to pieces. They threw his head and lyre into a river. The spirit of Orpheus was at last liberated and rushed to reunite with his beloved Eurydice in the underworld, where he blissfully lives on, eternally in her presence.

According to the sixth-century philosopher Proclus, one of the final deans of the Platonic Acadamy, Greek theology was thoroughly grounded in the mystical doctrine of Orpheus.[2] The Greek savior/redeemer is credited with inventing the alphabet and imparting names to the gods of the Greek pantheon, names that, in their gematria, reflected numbers associated with the harmonious workings of the cosmos that he revealed to the Pythagoreans.

The Christian patriarch Clement of Alexandria (A.D. 150–216) saw a deep connection between Jesus and Orpheus, describing Jesus as the New Orpheus and suggesting that Christianity was the New Song of the cosmos. Clement perceived Christianity as a marriage of Greek philosophy conveying the universal wisdom of priests and sages of antiquity with the prophetic tradition and ethical system of Judaism, a union now manifested in a new celestial harmony of Christianity. The mystical cult of Orpheus had much in common with Christianity: Both taught of a divine spark in human beings and the mystical resurrection of the god/hero; both taught spiritual transformation of their initiates, victory over death, and the afterlife of the spirit, and both are connected with fishes and with the image of the Good Shepherd.[3] The gods of both cults are saviors who visit the underworld to bring back souls of the dead. One artifact dating from circa A.D. 300 depicts Orpheus on a cross, similar to the one on which Jesus was crucified. Another shows Jesus playing a lyre with the wild animals resting at his feet in a mode made familiar by depictions of Orpheus, who charmed the wild animals with his music. One interpretation of this common image is that the animals represent the signs of the zodiac[4]—the stars and eons enchanted into harmonious and orderly precession by the song of the Savior—creating the music of the spheres. One is reminded of the messianic age prophesied by Isaiah, when the calf and the lion shall browse together (Isaiah 11:6). Formed in classical traditions, many educated converts to Christianity embraced a view of Jesus as the new incarnation of the beloved and familiar spirit of Orpheus.

A further connection between the Orphic tradition and Christianity is found in the use of symbolic numbers throughout the sacred texts of the Christian scriptures. Legend claimed that Orpheus had discovered the canon of sacred numbers underlying all creation and had imparted this knowledge to the Pythagoreans, who passed it down to initiates of their academy. The remnants of this once universal system of numbers are seen in the architecture of Greek temples and other classical structures, as well as in more ancient monuments, including Stonehenge and the Egyptian pyramids.[5] The same symbolic numbers of the sacred canon are encoded by gematria into important passages of their literature—treatises of Plato and the Hebrew Bible among them. Because the alphabet letters were used also as numbers in both Hebrew and Greek, the names, titles, and phrases of the sacred texts were carefully coined to yield sums that reflected cosmic principles underlying all creation. This ancient tradition of setting phrases to number was carried on by the authors of the New Testament—the gospels, epistles, and Book of Revelation—and is the subject of *Magdalene's Lost Legacy*.

Eurydice and Mary Magdalene

While the Christian fathers drew a connection between Jesus and Orpheus, apparently no one felt moved to connect Mary Magdalene with Eurydice. Having forgotten that Mary and Jesus represent the archetypal beloveds, interpreters of this similar myth fail to notice that Eurydice, bearer of the wounded feminine, is attacked by a male assailant, then bitten by a poisonous viper, dies, and is committed to the underworld. She represents womankind, vulnerable to male aggression and superior strength, and is victim of a second fate when she tries to flee the first. When the savior Orpheus comes to redeem his wife in her injured condition, he almost succeeds in winning her freedom, but at the last moment, forgetting the demand that he not look back, he tragically loses her. Brokenhearted, Orpheus manages to bring truths and secrets back from the underworld, gifts for humanity, but he is doomed to a lonely life of celibacy—stripped of his beloved partner—until he himself is murdered and torn to shreds. The reunion of the lovers is realized only in the afterlife.

In an earlier chapter, we noted that Jesus was a champion of the feminine, treating women with concern and respect unparalleled in the society of his era. One clear goal of his earthly mission appears to have been healing the unclean and disenfranchised, as expressed in various parables and stories about women in the gospels. Some suggest that Jesus was the prototypical feminist, determined to include women in his message of hope and reconciliation. In my view, the underlying mission of Jesus—as the incarnation of the sacred bridegroom—was to raise and embrace the feminine in his sacred union with Mary Magdalene, restoring at all levels the paradigm of equal partnership and the balance of masculine and feminine energies indigenous to the planet Earth, but so long denied in the experience of the human family.

The story of Orpheus and Eurydice haunts Christianity and is incorporated into its own mythology: Orpheus is prevented from living in happy union with his bride on the earthly plane. In the end, he must leave her behind in Tartarus and wait to be reunited with her in the afterlife. The Christ couple in the Easter garden echoes the tragic separation of its Orphic predecessors. Like Eurydice, Mary Magdalene reaches to embrace her beloved, calling out his name, but the two are forced to separate. Jesus must ascend to the celestial plane alone, leaving Mary to suffer political exile on the physical plane and denigration and defilement in myth and allegory. Both Orpheus and Jesus bring great gifts for their followers—secrets of transformation and enlightenment—and in both myths, union with the beloved is denied. Both Eurydice and Mary Magdalene are left behind. Orpheus returns alone to the earth realm, while Jesus ascends to a heavenly throne—alone—where he manifests the ascendant male principle of Western civilization for the next two thousand years.

The Greco-Roman world that created these myths of eternal separation was thoroughly committed to the superiority of the reason-based solar/masculine principle and was unable to envision a true partnership of the wounded, denigrated feminine Sophia with the solar Logos/god-hero. This milieu was the same society that accepted the deduction of Aristotle that women were mere incubators of male seed—their only contributions to the embryo being physical matter and the field in which it grew. Following the precepts of Plato, who thought that females were degenerate human beings and that only males were created directly by the gods and possessed souls, a number of early fathers of Christianity also denied that women had souls. In his treatise *Panarion* (79.1), Epiphanius (315–403) writes that women are a feeble race, untrustworthy and of mediocre intelligence, a view that echoed sentiments expressed by the Greek philosophers. In Epistle 1 Timothy, the author, erroneously assumed to be Paul, does not allow women to teach or to have authority over men, while another epistle insists that women are to be obedient to their husbands: "Let wives be subject to their husbands as to the Lord because a husband is head of the wife . . ." (Ephesians 4:22–23).

The Sophia Myth

It seems odd, then, in light of their apparent misogyny, to discover that two early philosophers, Pythagoras and Parmenides, had a passionate relationship with Sophia, whom they perceived as Goddess, the manifestation of the Wisdom of God. Yet numerous texts from antiquity suggest that the Sophia was so honored. Different groups characterized her in different ways: She was the first creation of the Divine, his delight and the mirror of his divinity, his spouse, his feminine counterpart or his manifestation. She was, alternatively, the bearer of feminine consciousness. King Solomon sought Wisdom (Sophia) as his "bride" and Pythagoras coined the word *philosopher* to mean "lover of Sophia." Among his school of Pythagoreans and their intellectual heirs, the Sophia was personified as a feminine entity, the source of enlightenment and inspiration. She survives in Christianity as the Holy Sophia, synonymous with the Holy Spirit. Sophia instructs her devotees in goodness, righteousness, and self-discipline. She reveals herself to those who desire to know her, and knowledge of her is sweeter than honey (Sirach 24:19). The gospel states: "[H]ow much more will the Father give the Good Spirit to those who ask him?" (Luke 11:13). In Hebrew and Aramaic the Spirit of God is feminine, not masculine as in later Western or Roman Christianity, where the Latin word *spiritus* is masculine.

A gnostic myth with close ties to Mary Magdalene's story is the myth of the fallen Sophia. This story of redemption can be read on two levels. It is the story of the collective feminine consciousness abased and denigrated in a male-dominated civilization and also of the individual soul in need of redemption. As outlined in chapter 4, Sophia, the favored daughter, left her celestial home, the house of her benevolent father, and willfully pursued her own desires, falling deeper and deeper into a life of sinful pleasures and vice. Eventually, she became so dissipated that she grew disgusted with her own behavior and finally cried out in desperation to her heavenly father. Immediately, he sent forth her brother/bridegroom Logos, with whom she was joyfully united in the bridal chamber—healed and made whole again—becoming her true spiritual self. Myth is not historical fact; it is a story that keeps repeating over and over, an archetypal pattern. The story of the soul's redemption and transformation, turning away from a life of dissipation and thirsting for spiritual enlightenment, is the essence of the Christian message, and both orthodox and heretical sects saw it embodied in Mary Magdalene. A number of early fathers of the Church recognized Mary Magdalene as the new Eve before that title was awarded to the Virgin Mary. In Mary Magdalene, Hippolytus of Rome recognized that what was lost by Eve through her disobedience in the Garden of Eden was restored in Mary of Bethany, called the Magdalene—"Eve has become apostle"![6]

Isis

Another myth containing elements of Magdalene's story is that of Isis, the great goddess of the Egyptians worshipped in the Roman Empire as queen of heaven and earth. Isis was the sister-bride of Osiris in the *hieros gamos* cult celebrating the growth, harvest, and regeneration of vegetation in the Nile valley. Osiris was the bringer of knowledge to the peoples of the earth: He taught them to plant and cultivate grain, to harvest fruit from trees, and to make wine and beer. He was universally loved and praised as a god, which caused his brother, Set, to become insanely jealous. At a dinner party, Osiris was persuaded to climb into a large chest built by his evil brother, who immediately had the coffer sealed and thrown into the Nile. After killing him, Set chopped Osiris into many pieces and scattered them far and wide. Isis, the bereft sister-bride of Osiris, set out to look for her beloved and miraculously conceived his child, Horus. After many adventures, she was able to reassemble most of the pieces of her husband and bury them with honor. Osiris became the god who guided the dead into resurrection and rebirth. His solar myth and cult hold numerous points in common with that of Jesus, and the story of Isis is in many ways reminiscent of Mary Magdalene, the bereaved spouse searching for her bridegroom.

The legends of Isis and Mary Magdalene are woven into a cult of the Black Madonna celebrated each year in Marseilles at the feast of Candlemas on February 2. Isis was often rendered black, so effigies of the black Virgin may trace their origins back to her mythology. Candlemas falls at the time of the pagan festival Imbolc, celebrating the quickening of the earth as warm shafts of the returning sunlight impregnate the fields and life begins to stir. In ancient times, women descended at this time into the dark interior of a cave and lit torches, then brought the fire out of the cave and torched the fields, burning off the chaff left from the former year's harvest. After this purification of the fields, it was time to sow new seed. In the Christian calendar, parallel to the ancient rites, Candlemas celebrates the "churching" or purification of the Virgin Mary forty days after the birth of her child, the period of postpartum rest and purification required by Jewish law. Centuries ago, in the cult of Isis celebrated in Marseilles, little boat-shaped cookies called *navettes* were baked in her honor, a reminder of her journeys in search of her lost husband, Osiris. In modern times, navettes are still baked at Candlemas, but now they honor the early Christians who brought the gospel to Gaul—the three Marys and their friends in the little boat with no oars. The city's dignitaries take the statue of the Black Madonna, Our Lady of the Witness, out of the crypt at Saint Victor's Basilica and carry it through the city streets.

The question is: Whom does this Black Madonna represent? Overtly, it is proclaimed that she is the Virgin Mary, whose Feast of the Purification is officially celebrated at Candlemas. But the Mary who is celebrated for having brought the gospel to Marseilles is not the Virgin, but rather the Magdalene. Like Isis, she is the bereaved bride of the hieros gamos mythology celebrated in the Song of Songs. And her blackness is the blackness of the bride in that same Canticle: "I am black but beautiful . . . swarthy from my labor in my brothers' vineyards" (Song of Songs 1:5–6). The blackness of the bride is symbolic of her connections to the Wisdom tradition and to the earth, but also of her obscurity and enforced exile—echoing that of Magdalene from Judaea in the first century and from our collective consciousness for nearly two millennia.

These myths and legends, calling to us from antiquity, hinting of the feminine partner lost, or denied, or wandering in search of her beloved, were known and loved by the Greek-speaking pagans of the Roman Empire. Surely they must have recognized Mary Magdalene in the role of the Lost Bride/Sophia/Isis. But the myth to which Mary Magdalene's story bears the strongest connection is the myth from another society—not of the pagan Hellenized empire of Rome, but of her own Jewish heritage.

The people who best recognized in Magdalene the archetypal bride were her own people, the Jews, whose prophets had styled Israel as the bride of Yahweh and whose stormy history had left the nation vulnerable to rape, pillage, and abject humiliation—occupied and exploited by victorious foreign armies. Let us examine the myth of Magdalene as it relates to the history and traditions of an abused and exiled people—of whom she becomes the prototype and representative par excellence.

The Goddess in Israel

Recent archaeological excavations in Israel confirm that the people there once worshipped a female goddess whom they characterized as the beloved consort of Yahweh himself. Thousands of little clay statues of the Asherah figurine, rotund in her aspect as a love and fertility goddess, have surfaced in Israel, attesting to the widespread cult of this goddess, whose worship took place in groves mentioned in several passages in the Hebrew Bible. No images of male deities in corresponding numbers were discovered, so it is apparent that the goddess Asherah was honored in her own right. When the disapproving prophets of Yahweh and the priests of the temple anathematized the goddess, her cult was officially extinguished, though people likely retained altars to the queen of heaven in their homes and continued to honor her in private. The prophet Jeremiah attempted to halt cultic practices honoring the goddess: "The children gather wood, and the fathers kindle the fire, and the women knead the dough, to make cakes to the queen of heaven, and to pour out drink offerings unto other gods, that they may provoke me to anger" (Jeremiah 7:18). The Jewish people were reluctant to give up their worship of the goddess. They responded to Jeremiah: "We will not listen to what you say in the name of the Lord. Rather will we continue doing what we had proposed; we will burn incense to the queen of heaven and pour out libations to her as we and our fathers, our kings and princes have done in the cities of Judah and the streets of Jerusalem. Then we had enough food to eat and we were well off. We suffered no misfortune" (Jeremiah 44: 16–17).

Later Hebrew tradition styles the Shekinah as the feminine counterpart of Yahweh, an aspect of himself with feminine attributes of beauty, compassion, gentleness, and kindness. She is his bride with whom he unites in the Holy of Holies in the Temple in Jerusalem. When the Temple was destroyed in A.D. 70, the Shekinah was forced from her bridal chamber and, like her people, was sent into exile, a perpetual wanderer in the wilderness, always longing to be united with her beloved. This story echoes lines we mentioned earlier. Taken from the prophet Micah, the passage proclaims the fate of the Magdal-eder—the stronghold of the Daughter of Sion. She is a metaphor for the entire nation of her people, weeping over the death of her king and counselor. She, too, must go into exile; she must dwell in the open fields. To Babylon must she go, and from there she shall be rescued (Micah 4:8–10). The single woman in the Common Era who embodies the myth of the Shekinah and the Diaspora of the Jewish people is the Mary called the Magdalene, the Magdal-eder—"watchtower" or "stronghold of the flock." She is the personification of the Holy City, the Daughter of Sion, and represents her land and people as the bride of the eternal bridegroom. He is the Good Shepherd, she the Watchtower of the Flock. The symbolism and the theme are mutually affirming of the sacred union at the heart of Judaism as well as that of Christianity.

The scriptures of the Jewish people record several historical periods of ignominious defeat, enslavement, and exile. Their initial displacement was in Egypt, where the sons of Jacob (Israel) labored in bondage to Pharaoh until Moses led them across the Red Sea in the thirteenth century B.C. Their nation was later defeated, in 586 B.C., by Babylonian armies. Many of her people were brought in chains to Babylon, where they remained in exile for more than half a century before finally returning to their homeland, under Persian hegemony, after the defeat of Babylon.

One of the most pathos-filled passages in all of ancient literature is the Book of Lamentations, from the Hebrew Bible. Written soon after the fall of Jerusalem to the Babylonians in the sixth century B.C., the first chapter describes the plight of the Holy City, here personified as the devastated Widow Sion: "How lonely she is now. . . . Widowed is she who was mistress over nations; the princess among the provinces has been made a toiling slave. Bitterly she weeps at night, tears upon her cheeks . . ." (Lamentations 1:1–2). The poet suggests that Jerusalem was punished for her sins—whoring after false gods and consorting with foreign allies, her "lovers," who defiled and then abandoned her. Now she is desolate, her walls in ruins, her domain a wasteland, her children starving in the streets. She is the habitat of bats and vermin. As we noted earlier, the Hebrew Bible often equates idolatry with prostitution in the extended metaphor of God's marriage covenant with his chosen people. The people have been unfaithful, whoring after pagan deities, but Yahweh their God is ever patient and forgiving, calling them to return. But now, his anger is inflamed and he allows the Babylonians to conquer and chastise his sinful bride. In Lamentations, she mourns her disastrous fate and that of her children, eventually moving Yahweh to restore her to favor as of old. We are reminded of Esther, pleading for her people before the throne of King Ahasuerus.

In 539 B.C., the Persian king Cyrus defeated the Babylonians and allowed Jewish slaves still in Babylonian exile to return to Jerusalem to rebuild their city. In the period that followed, prophets and priests worked to establish a theocracy centered on Temple worship, purifying the nation and expelling foreign influence, while insisting on the strict monotheism expressed in the books of their postexilic prophets. By 516 B.C., the Temple in Jerusalem had been rebuilt and later, under the supervision of Nehemiah in the mid-fifth century B.C., the walls of Jerusalem had been restored along with the integrity of the nation.

But barely a hundred years later, in 333 B.C., the Jewish nation was once again conquered by foreigners, this time by the armies of Alexander the Great. There followed a century of bloody battles between rival Greek claimants to the region, during which time Koiné (Greek) became the prevailing language of the region, and Greek thought and customs strongly influenced the occupied territory. Jewish freedom fighters wrested their people from Greek rule under the leadership of the Maccabees, patriots "zealous for the Law of Israel," establishing the Hasmonean dynasty, which ruled over an independent Jewish nation for the next century (160–63 B.C.), but quarrels between royal heirs paved the way for Roman conquest of the province of Palestine in 63 B.C. In 37 B.C., King Herod, a foreigner and pagan by birth and preference whose first wife was the popular royal Hasmonean princess Mariamne, was installed on the throne in Jerusalem, a puppet of the Roman emperor and despised by the Jews he ruled.

The Jews also abhorred the pagan shrines and idols erected in their country by foreign rulers; they rebelled on several occasions, attempting to rid their country of its overlords. At one point in these confrontations, Jewish rebels stoned Roman legionnaires. Retribution was fierce: The

Roman general Varus ordered two thousand Jewish patriots crucified and their bodies left to rot for days along the road from Jerusalem to Galilee.

At Jesus' time, Palestine was a conquered province, Jerusalem an occupied city. Faithful Jews despised the temple priests and ruling Herodian tetrarchs, corrupt and dissipated heirs of Herod the Butcher, who collaborated shamelessly with the Romans. Out of this crucible were born the reformed "sister" faiths of Christianity and Pharisaical Judaism. The people of Judaea were in anguish—suffering every indignity and malaise of a nation under military occupation by a foreign conqueror. Roman horsemen ran down pedestrians in the streets of Jerusalem, overturned vendors' tables in the market square, raped local wives and daughters, demanded taxes, confiscated property, and worshipped effigies of their emperor as divine. Their herds of pigs, an unclean animal, were an affront to the Jews, as was the aroma of their roasted pork. The entire populace of Judaea may have felt themselves possessed by demons—demons of rage, frustration, and depression. They longed for the promised Davidic Messiah to rid them of the humiliation and tyranny of Roman rule.

By the time the first gospel was written to record the teachings and ministry of Jesus, the Jewish nation had rebelled once again (A.D. 66–70), and their uprising had been crushed. Roman soldiers forced Jewish men to cast the stones from the temple walls one by one into the streets below. The Holy City—Daughter of Sion, princess among the provinces—was once again in ruins, her people banished from within its walls, sent out to "dwell in the fields." Once again, Yahweh had hidden his face from them, allowing their enemies to defeat and enslave them, to destroy and humiliate them.

Of all the women in the scriptures, who was it that, for the first-century authors of the gospels, embodied the metaphor of the abandoned bride—the personification of the beloved community—now scorned and vilified, sent into remote exile, fleeing the voracious beast that threatens to devour her? Who is physically removed from dangers that beset her, sent away to safety with her newborn infant in a faraway land, and abandoned there in relative obscurity for centuries? Mary Magdalene, bearing the archetype of ekklesia (Church) and Widow of

Sion was so thoroughly lost in her exile that the apocalyptic visionary, probably himself unaware that her child was not a son, symbolically envisions her offspring (and eventual dynasty) as a male "who will rule with an iron rod." Magdalene herself embodies both the historical reality and the ongoing metaphor of this woman: the Widow Sion (from Micah 4:8–10 and Lamentations) in exile—the abandoned queen of a devastated and disconsolate nation, the Shekinah.

One powerful and widely recognized image of this archetype is the ninth-century icon of the Black Madonna, Our Lady of Czestochowa, who bears a scar on her right cheek, the fulfillment of an ancient prophecy: "With a rod they strike on the cheek the ruler of Israel" (Micah 4:14). In the painting *The Way to Calvary,* by Simone Martini, Mary Magdalene bears a similar scar on her right cheek. Massive behind her are the walls and the gate with twin towers—the ramparts of Jerusalem. The twin towers are a symbol for the Holy City as bride found, once again, in the Hebrew Song of Songs: "I am a wall and my breasts are towers" (fig. 6.1).

This, then, is the tradition from which Mary Magdalene stems, the myth of the chosen people as bride of Yahweh in a relationship that was perceived as a marriage covenant. As the royal representative of her land and people, Mary called the Magdalene, a sister of Lazarus, anoints

Fig. 6.1. A medieval watermark representing the twin towers and gate of the Holy City. The J is for Jerusalem.

Jesus and proclaims him the messianic King. As Christ incarnates the masculine Divine as bridegroom, Mary Magdalene embodies the people of Israel as bride. Remembering that the New Testament gospels call Jesus a *tekton*, which means "architect" and "construction engineer" as well as "carpenter," we now more fully appreciate the prophecy of Isaiah that speaks of Yahweh's relationship with Israel—the marriage covenant embodied in the Christ couple:

> For *the Lord delights in you*
> *and makes your land his spouse.*
> *As a young man marries a virgin*
> *Your builder shall marry you;*
> *And as a bridegroom rejoices in his bride*
> *So shall your God rejoice in you.*
>
> Isaiah 62:4b–5

7

The Beloved Espoused

And I saw the holy city, New Jerusalem, arrayed as
a bride adorned for her husband.

In his *Answer to Job,* the mystic psychologist-philosopher Carl Jung makes a comment that sums up the need to restore the human bride of the human Jesus to our collective experience. In discussing the archetypal bridegroom of Christianity and his bride, Jung writes that the "equality" of the couple "requires to be metaphysically anchored in the figure of a 'divine' woman, the Bride of Christ."[1] Jung insists further that just as the human, physical bridegroom Christ cannot be replaced by an institution, the bride needs to be a personal representation in a human form. We cannot envision a human Jesus embracing a building—church or city—full of people; the image must be rejected as incongruous. If we are to envision a historical Jesus embracing a bride, she cannot be a mere metaphor. What we *can* envision is Jesus embracing a woman—his Domina counterpart—who represents her people, the ekklesia. In the Apocalypse, the bride descends from heaven to celebrate her nuptials (Revelation 21:2). She is the human embodiment of the Holy City, the New Jerusalem. And the goal of Christian theology is her sacred marriage with the eternal bridegroom.

The gospels of the New Testament provide us with a woman

perceived to represent the community in its perpetual expectancy and hope for fulfillment of the millennial prophecies, when God will dwell in their midst. The only consistent candidate for this role of bride is Mary, the sister of Lazarus, called the Magdalene. Any possible confusion about the identity of Mary Magdalene was set to rest when Pope Gregory I proclaimed in a sermon delivered in 591 that Mary Magdalene was the sinful woman who anointed Jesus; John's gospel names her Mary, the sister of Lazarus. In all probability, the pope was not making a controversial statement; he was articulating a belief already widely held in Western Europe, where churches built in honor of Mary Magdalene were frequent and her historical presence celebrated. She was one of the most popular of all Christian saints and her image the one most often painted by medieval artists, with one exception only—that of the Virgin and Child, an image illustrating the prevailing doctrine of the Theotokos honored in the East.

Mistaken Identities

In Western European art, Mary Magdalene's image became inextricably compounded with two other female saints popular in medieval times—Saint Mary of Egypt and Saint Barbara—the former, by virtue of her legend, and the latter, by association with her iconography. Each of these probably fictional saints offers valuable insight into the medieval faces of Mary Magdalene.

Saint Mary of Egypt, or Mary Gyp, as she was affectionately known, was a prostitute whose story was brought back from the Middle East in the twelfth century by returning Crusaders. The soldiers apparently found in her a sympathetic patroness who looked with leniency on sexual indiscretions. Her legend asserts that Mary of Egypt was a third-century prostitute who obtained passage to Palestine by offering to ply her profession on board the ship. Upon arrival in the Holy Land, she converted to Christianity and gave up promiscuity, living out the rest of her life as a desert hermit. Her story, like that of Mary Magdalene, is found in the thirteenth-century *Golden Legend* of Jacobus de Voragine. One of the miracles associated with the dark Mary the Egyptian was ascension of her body into heaven, a favor extended to the Virgin Mary but also to Mary Magdalene by artists who confused her story with that of the Egyptian prostitute. Both Marys are said to have been harlots, both repented and were converted to Christ, both became hermits for the final decades of their lives. A further confusion in their stories is the child/servant Sarah, also called "the Egyptian," said to have been among the party of Christian exiles who traveled to Gaul with Mary Magdalene. Apparently, some features from tales of the Egyptian prostitute, blackened by the relentless desert sun during her years in isolation and stripped naked as her clothes gradually disintegrated, were projected onto Mary Magdalene by medieval devotees. We could speculate that the emaciated Mary Magdalene effigy of Donatello (1389–1466) might have been inspired as easily by the story of Mary the Egyptian as by that of Mary Magdalene, who, it is said, lived for thirty years on the Eucharist wafers brought daily to her mountain cave by angels, one of the colorful details found in the account of her life published in the *Golden Legend*.

In 2002, I spent part of an afternoon in the Chapel of the Most Holy Trinity at West Point, New York—the chapel in which I was baptized as an infant and in which the Emmanuel prayer community was formed in 1973. I decided to examine images of Mary Magdalene in the chapel that was my spiritual home for so many years of my life. At first I was dismayed. Looking carefully at each stained-glass window, noting its scriptural or historic reference, no image of Mary Magdalene appeared present in any of the scenes. Just as I was leaving, disappointed, I glanced over my right shoulder at the stained-glass window behind me and felt prickles down my neck. There she was after all, standing regal in a magnificent mosaic of colored shards, gleaming in the spring sunshine.

As I looked more closely at her image, I recognized that Mary Magdalene was suffering once again from a case of mistaken identity. Standing in her sunlit window, she held a tower in her arms. A chalice was depicted below the image, while the inscription identified the woman as Saint Barbara. But the tower and chalice are associated with Mary, whose title is derived from the Aramaic word for "tower" and whose legend claims that she brought the Holy Grail to Europe. Often Saint Barbara wears the symbols of martyrdom in medieval iconography, but a crown is also a universally accepted symbol for royalty. In fact, a crown with numerous points originally represented the turrets and ramparts of a walled city, symbolically placed on the head of its patroness or protector. A famous early example of this artistic representation is the relief carving of the Great Goddess dating from the Roman period. She wears a replica of the city of Aix on her head—the prototypical crown.

In 1969, when the Roman Catholic Church revised its official calendar of saints' feasts, Saint Barbara was summarily dropped, her story deemed spurious. Sealed in a tower, the third-century Barbara had been so eager to become a Christian—or so the story claimed—that she let down her hair so that a priest could climb up to bring her the gospel and the Eucharist, a story strongly reminiscent of the heroine in the European fairy tale Rapunzel. Barbara's father, an important Syrian official, was so angry at Barbara's profession of Christianity that he ordered his own beautiful daughter beheaded. On his way home from the execution, he was struck by a bolt of lightning and killed. Combining various elements of this legend, Barbara became the patron saint of military engineers and artillerymen, miners, masons, and firefighters, protecting them from sudden death by fire or explosion. The name Barbara means "foreign woman." Her bizarre legend first circulated in Europe during the seventh century, contemporaneous with Merovingian rule in the northern regions of France. It gained popularity in the ninth and tenth centuries, when legends of the Holy Grail emerged in the oral tradition, though not yet written, and continued throughout the Middle Ages.

But, as in many medieval stories about the saints, details of Saint Barbara's legend seem contrived, though they may hold a fossil of truth, as so many legends do. I think it probable that an artisan or artist created an image of a Mary Magdalene with her traditional long hair, a tower (derived from the root word of her honorific—*magdala*), a Grail chalice, and a royal crown. People unfamiliar with Hebrew might not have recognized the image as a rendering of Mary Magdalene, Grail bearer and ekklesia, so the iconography could easily have been misunderstood, and perhaps years later someone generated a legend to match the icon—ex post facto naming the woman Barbara and creating the bizarre story, now rejected by the Church, to explain the long hair, the tower, the chalice, and the crown. As the now revised story was told and retold and the icon copied in various forms, shapes, and sizes, the legend of Saint Barbara proliferated, veiling the original connection with Mary Magdalene. I am convinced that Saint Barbara was a cover story invented to protect Mary Magdalene and her connection with the Grail and its heresy. We are lifting its veil.

Another anomaly remains associated with the icon of the Grail and the long hair associated with Mary Magdalene. Christian paintings, but also statues standing along the outer walls of Gothic cathedrals at Chartres, Freibourg, and other European cities, often present a figure who symbolizes Christianity. She wears a crown and carries a chalice, and she may hold a banner emblazoned with a cross. In paintings, the cross is red on a white background. The figure personifies the Church, the bride of Christ. The crown proclaims her as royal bride and the chalice she holds is supposed to be symbolic of the Eucharistic meal. The Christian icon appears related to Barbara/Magdalene iconography, remembering that it was Magdalene who represented ekklesia, beloved bride of Christ, among earliest Christian exegetes.

The painting *Saint Magdalen* (plate 13) by Segna di Buonaventure (d. 1331) shows her holding what looks like a tower rather than her traditional alabaster jar. She provides what I consider a missing link between Barbara and the Magdalene.[2] She was also a *barbara*, a "foreign woman," banished into exile in a faraway land. Her first exile was historical—the journey in a fragile boat across the Mediterranean Sea from her homeland. Her second was metaphorical—enforced exile from her rightful position throughout two millennia of Christianity. Because the feminine principle was no longer honored in the power-drunk cultural milieu of the Roman Empire, women were not honored, and because women were not honored, this woman was not honored. The historic reality mirrors the pattern established and enthroned in the Roman solar- or masculine-oriented value system.

Often artists do not supply titles for their paintings, leaving it to viewers to identify a scene or character by means of associated icons. We can see an example of a misidentification in the fifteenth-century painting from the Flemish school depicting a woman identified as Saint Barbara (plate 14). Painted by Robert Campin, the saint bears a strong resemblance to the image of Mary Magdalene in a painting by the artist's contemporary Rogier van der Weyden (plate 15). The women in these works are depicted in nearly identical poses: Each is seated, reading a book, symbolic of Sophia/Wisdom in iconography; each is wearing a dark green gown, symbolic of fertility, over a gold brocade underskirt, the raiment of the bride. Robert Campin's Saint Barbara has the long wavy hair often associated with Mary Magdalene, while the hair of Rogier van der Weyden's Magdalene is hidden under her coif. The alabaster jar universally associated with Mary Magdalene is seen in the foreground of Rogier van der Weyden's work, whereas the flask of ointment in the Campin painting is standing on a shelf to the right above the fireplace. A lily in a vase near the woman in Campin's work is the symbol of the bride in the Song of Songs, where the bridegroom proclaims, "As a lily among thorns, so is my beloved among women" (Song of Songs 2:2). Art critics over the centuries hold that the lily is a symbol for the Virgin Mary and her perpetual purity, but the bridegroom in the Canticle speaks of it as a simile for his beloved, not his mother.

I believe that in Robert Campin's painting, the woman with curly auburn hair is Mary Magdalene rather than Saint Barbara. The tower seen through the window belongs to the iconography of both women, but only the Magdalene is associated with the flask of ointment. The Xs in the upper portion of the window are vaguely suspicious; X is the common symbol of the alternative, underground version of Christianity that acknowledged Mary Magdalene as the *dompna* (lady) of their Domine—Christ himself. We noted similar Xs in the transom of the window in Tintoretto's *Christ in the House of Martha and Mary* (see plate 12).

The Tragic Divorce

The enforced separation of the beloveds in Christian mythology amounts to the "great divorce," which is thrice tragic when we realize that it was perpetrated for millennia by the preeminent and most powerful institution in Western civilization. The Roman Catholic Church abhors divorce, quoting and upholding gospel passages Mark 10:2–9 and Matthew 19:3–9, in which Jesus insists on the absolute sanctity of monogamous marriage. The ongoing ramifications of this enforced separation of the archetypal Christ couple to our culture are enormous—ultimately the domain of the wounded king denied his feminine partner becomes a wasteland, its towns in ruins, its citizens in misery. There is no justice, no peace, no hope in a domain where the leaders—the anointed and ordained shepherds—busily shepherd themselves instead of the sheep (Ezekiel 34:8).

At several periods during these two Christian millennia, the story of the beloveds at the heart of the gospel story was poised to break forth from the underground stream of mystics, artists, and intellectuals who were its perennial custodians. But each time the story surfaced, it was squelched, declared heretical, and again forced underground. When it surfaced among the twelfth- and thirteenth-century Cathars and their troubadours, it was brutally suppressed by the dungeon, fire, and sword of the Inquisition, formed in 1239 for that purpose, though Grail legends that sprang from the heresy gained popularity and were widely disseminated in medieval Europe.

Today, under attack by clergy and volunteer defenders of the faith who vehemently deny (or ignore) powerful circumstantial evidence supporting the sacred union, the story of the Christ couple is labeled fiction or bunk. What a pity that these modern-day heirs of the guardians of the walls who piously assaulted the bride of the Canticle, who beat her and stripped her of her mantle (a euphemism for rape in their culture), are still—even now!—bitterly determined to keep the bride from being reunited with her bridegroom. Jesus was separated from his beloved partner at the dawn of the new age of Pisces, when the gospels were yet new. How joyful will be their eventual reunion!

Perhaps the zealous guardians of today, eager to debunk the sacred marriage, should reread a story found in the Book of Acts. A respected teacher of the law, Gamaliel warned Jewish elders of the ruling council, the Sanhedrin, not to try to silence the apostles preaching the good news in the streets of Jerusalem: "[I]f this work is of men, it will be overcome, but if it is of God, you will not be able to overthrow it. Else you may find yourselves fighting even against God" (Acts 5:38).

Over the centuries, groups of enlightened and intuitive European artists and poets occasionally connected with the underground stream and the story of the forgotten bride. Artists from all over Western Europe used heretical symbols in their paintings, a fact that suggests they passed down the great secret of the fully human, married Christ from one generation to another, a subject discussed in greater depth in *The Woman with the Alabaster Jar*. In that book, I gave powerful evidence for the existence of the Grail heresy, concentrating on medieval and Renaissance artworks, artifacts, and folklore. I did not include an important but much later circle of artists and poets inspired by the Grail legends—the brotherhood of the Pre-Raphaelites, formed in the mid-nineteenth century by Dante Gabriel Rosetti and his close friends. This celebrated group is familiar to many as Victorian naturalist-romantics. Though not directly linked with the heretical Church of Amor, their paintings include lovely scenes from the Grail legends and various pieces with moral or tragic themes, often with ethereal women—goddesses of beauty and love from Arthurian legend and pagan myth.

Poetry created within this circle of gifted friends often focuses on religious topics, and some of the artists appear captivated by the legends and inspiration of Mary Magdalene. Several works of the Pre-Raphaelites depict Mary Magdalene, including Dante Gabriel Rossetti's *Mary Magdalene* (plate 16), a striking redhead robed in dark green, shown holding a large egg. His painting *The Beloved* (plate 17) depicts another ravishing redhead—the bride from the Song of Songs. Other paintings of the Pre-Raphaelites concentrate on the Grail legends and these (why are we not surprised?) contain a number of knights wearing capes and tunics emblazoned with red Xs—the primary symbol that identifies alternative Christian adherents of the Church of the Grail.

Fossils of the secret tradition—the major arcana expressed in symbol in medieval watermarks and in tarot trumps of the earliest decks—survived and resurfaced in Victorian England among this visionary and inspired brotherhood of poet-painters. Many paintings of other Pre-Raphaelites, especially those of John William Waterhouse, focus on the feminine as archetype or goddess—surrounded by roses or lilies, with copious red hair and flowing garments—while their sonnets and other poems enhance this idealization of the beloved, often in a medieval context. Were these painters heretics or merely passionate devotees of the feminine as beloved?

Lady Greensleeves

A medieval Flemish master painted Mary Magdalene preaching the gospel, with people gathered around her in a woodsy setting (plate 18). Dressed in a brocade gown embroidered with vines, she shares her message of hope and regeneration. The boat in which she sailed to the shores of Gaul is visible in the distance. This painting touches on several themes connected with Mary Magdalene: There is no church in the picture; Magdalene cannot preach from a church pulpit, but only out in the open, as was the case for medieval "heretics" and reformers who met at night in secluded areas to share their faith. Artists from the Netherlands (the Low Countries) were particularly aware of clandestine practice of their faith because of the repressive measures of the Spanish Inquisition imposed upon them during the sixteenth-century rule of the Spanish monarchs Charles V and Philip II. Mary Magdalene represented those outside the Church in their struggle for intellectual and religious freedom. The vine motif of her gown is the ubiquitous reminder of the theme of regeneration associated with the feminine she embodies, the raiment of the messianic bride from Psalm 45. It also echoes the words of Jesus in John 15: "I am the vine, you are the branches" (15:5), and shows the continuity of Mary Magdalene with the fruitful message of the gospel she preaches.

While many medieval portrayals of Mary Magdalene show her dressed in crimson or gold brocade—sometimes both—a large number of artists, including Dante Rossetti and Agnolo Bronzino (see plate 24), chose to dress the lady in green, the color associated with fertility and renewal, as in the *veriditas,* or principle of "greening," expressed in the poetry and other works of Hildegard von Bingen. Indeed, Mary Magdalene is often shown wearing maternity clothes and obviously pregnant. Her green gown apparently cloaks an advanced pregnancy in *The Resurrection of Lazarus,* by Geertgen tot Sint Jans (see plate 7); and in *Mary Magdalene,* the left panel of Rogier van der Weyden's Braque family triptych *Mary Magdalene* (see plate 6), she is wearing a tunic that laces up the front. Given that medieval women did not own many gowns, this was a typical medieval maternity garment, easily adjusted to accommodate advancing stages of pregnancy. The gold brocade and red Xs so often associated with Mary Magdalene and her great secret are displayed on the sleeves of her blouse.

Several "penitent Magdalene" works by Georges de la Tour, painted between 1636 and 1644, also show a woman in advancing stages of pregnancy, culminating in *The Penitent Magdalene* (or *Magdalene and the Two Flames*—plate 19). Because the twin flames are an esoteric symbol for the beloveds as soul mates and partners, the meaning of the painting seems clear. Lying on the table near her is a large, irregular pearl of great price, a metaphor for the Kingdom of God. Like Magdalene herself, the pearl was hidden—so long and so deep—that no one realized it was gone or had any clue to search for it. One of the earlier de la Tour paintings of Mary Magdalene, *Repenting Magdalene* (or *Magdalene of Night Light*—plate 20), appears in the Disney movie *The Little Mermaid,* at the bottom of the ocean in the Little Mermaid's treasure trove. It has been salvaged from a sunken galleon—"deep-sixed" like the Magdalene herself, her voice stolen when she was called prostitute. Another Magdalene painting, Piero della Francesca's majestic fifteenth-century fresco in the Arezzo Cathedral, portrays a massive woman dressed in a green gown partially covered by a red and white cape. While green denotes fertility, red and white represent passion and purity, attributes that are not mutually exclusive—but are most desirable!—in a bride.

Very often Mary Magdalene appears to be associated with fertility and the promise of regeneration and renewal. As a fully human and

PLATE 17: Dante Gabriel
Rossetti (1828–1882), *The
Beloved*. Tate Gallery, London.
Courtesy of Erich Lessing/
Art Resource, NY.

PLATE 18: Netherlandish (active c. 1480–
1520), *Saint Mary Magdalene Preaching*. John G.
Johnson Collection, 1917, Philadephia Museum
of Art, Philadelphia.

PLATE 19: Georges de la Tour (1593–1652), *The Penitent Magdalene* (or *Magdalene and the Two Flames*). Metropolitan Museum of Art, New York.

PLATE 20: Georges de la
Tour (1593–1652), *Repenting
Magdalene* (or *Magdalene
of Night Light*). Louvre, Paris.
Courtesy of Scala/
Art Resource, NY.

MARY·HATH·CHOSEN·THAT·GOOD·PART·WHICH
SHALL·NOT·BE·TAKEN·AWAY·FROM·HER

Erected to the Glory of God in loving memory of
Mary Forrest of Ardow. Died 23rd October, 1904,
by her affectionate sister, Isabella D. Forrest
Watson of Ardow.

PLATE 21: Stephen Adam
(d. 1910), stained-glass
window, Kilmore Church,
Dervaig, Isle of Mull,
Scotland. Photograph
courtesy of John Shuster.

PLATE 22: Jonathan Weber, *Mary Magdalene*.
Copyright © 2004 by Jonathan Weber.

PLATE 23: Patricia K. Ballantine, *Sacred Union*. Courtesy of Patricia K. Ballantine, "The Creative Flame."

PLATE 24: Agnolo di Cosimo
Bronzino (1503–1572),
Noli Me Tangere. Musée des Beaux-
Arts, Besançon. Courtesy of Scala/
Art Resource, NY.

full-bodied bearer of this archetypal principle, she fosters a deep connection with our flesh and blood, with our physical world, and with all creation, becoming the special patroness of those who would protect the environment and resources of the planet for future generations. While many of the Black Madonnas of France and Spain are dressed in gold, one notable exception is *Notre Dame de la Confessione* (Our Lady of the Witness) at Saint Victor's Basilica in Marseilles, where she is dressed in an emerald green cloak and wears a brooch in the shape of a fleur-de-lis, symbol of French royalty.

Green is associated with fertility, and the () shape called the vesica piscis—Mary Magdalene's geometric symbol—bears the same meaning: the womb of creativity, the matrix and doorway of life. The shape is replicated in leaves of numerous species of plants as well as in eggs and seeds: Almonds were sacred to the love goddess of the ancient world. A frequent artistic depiction of Christ shows the Savior enthroned within a mandorla, the vesica piscis often interpreted as a Christian symbol for the Holy Spirit or the Sophia, derived from its ancient associations with the goddess. This is a visual representation of Jesus' anointing by Sophia/Holy Wisdom herself, manifested by his actual anointing by the bride bearing the alabaster jar in the gospels, in obvious contradiction to the previously cited claim made by Pope John Paul II that Jesus was never externally anointed."[3]

Green is associated with hope, regeneration, and transformation, as well. A favorite medieval incarnation of the Lady of the Green as Mother Nature is found in Maid Marion, the companion of Robin Hood in the green wood of Merry Olde England. The popular folk hero and his bride provide yet another legend of sacred union and the "greening" principle that resonates within us. They mirror the King and Queen of the May, whose crowning culminated fertility rites that celebrated the vernal regeneration of the life force. Revelries in their honor included dancing around the phallic Maypole and making love in the woods and fields during festivals of Beltane, once celebrated on May first throughout Europe.

The verb *to marry* was derived from a nautical term meaning "to braid." But its ancient etymology is also interesting: In Indo-European, a *meri* was a young wife and a *meryo* was a young man, whence in Sanskrit was derived *maryo,* a young man or suitor. The Latin verb *maritare,* meaning "to marry," was the source of the Old French *marier* and Middle English *marien.* I find it enlightening that this word has *her* name on it—taken so for granted that we never pause to think of it. Neither is *merry,* meaning "joyful," so very far removed from the bower of the beloveds.

The folk also retained the memory of the "ever green One"—the regenerative masculine principle—in their legends and festivals, equating that principle with Christ himself and incorporating it with the pagan custom of bringing in a fresh evergreen conifer or pine to celebrate the rebirth of the sun at the winter solstice. We call it a Christmas tree, but its triangular shape is the archetypal symbol for the primal One, the creative masculine energy of the cosmos. The "green man" who peeks out of foliage in various relief carvings in walls and pillars of medieval churches is a hidden aspect of that same concept of the "ever green" life force incarnate in Christ, whose full humanity was denied by the Roman Church, but who embodied the principle of regeneration and vitality in the eyes of the people—creation in all its diverse manifestations.

A poignant theme of regeneration and reunion is celebrated in the *Hunt of the Unicorn* series (early sixteenth century), displayed in the Cloisters in New York City. In this series of six panels, the unicorn is savagely hunted and destroyed, but in a seventh panel (probably not one of the original series), he is seen frolicking in the enclosed garden, a metaphor for the bride in the Song of Songs: "You are a garden enclosed, my sister, my bride, a garden enclosed, a fountain sealed" (Song of Songs 4:12). Flowers and herbs symbolic of love, marriage, and fertility surround the unicorn, and pomegranate juice drips from the tree above him, again reminiscent of the Song of Songs, where the beloveds tryst in the orchard of pomegranates.[4] On the trunk of the pomegranate tree under which the unicorn rests two Xs are visible, formed by ropes attached to the initials *A* and *E* above his head. Double Xs were an important symbol for the alternative Christians who honored the sacred feminine, and occur often among their watermarks. Placed side-by-side and touching, the Xs form the rebus XX, the intertwined Λ and V symbols used to represent Ave Maria and Ave Millennium, two of their most significant slogans. The symbol of the compass and T-square, whose meaning is the quest for truth and enlightenment, was later adopted by the Brotherhood of Freemasons as its identifying logo.

The Nuptials of the Lamb

Although the movement itself was short-lived, lasting only about a decade, the style and influence of the Pre-Raphaelites spread well into the twentieth century. In 1906, on the Isle of Mull, situated off the west coast of Scotland, a church was erected to Saint Mary in the little town of Dervaig. The townspeople worked diligently to create their Kilmore (Church of Mary), designed to be the center of their worship. One of the beautiful stained-glass windows of the Kilmore is of special interest in our study of the many faces of Mary Magdalene (plate 21). The mosaic of brightly colored glass depicts the Christ couple celebrating their nuptials. They are "hand-fasted"—their right hands clasped—a widely recognized symbol for marriage still used in the marriage rite of some Christian denominations. The stained-glass window clearly portrays the nuptials of the Lamb and his bride, the Holy City, prophesied in the Book of Revelation. Behind the bridal couple standing in the doorway loom the twin towers, the medieval symbol representing the ramparts of Jerusalem.[5]

In the ancient rites of the sacred marriage, the bride represented and was identified with her land, her city and villages, her people. Often in the Hebrew Bible, as we have noted, the phrase "Daughter of Sion" refers to Jerusalem, the city, but also to the entire Jewish nation. In later doctrine, the title Daughter of Sion was one of those transferred to Mary, the mother of Jesus, but here in the window, the Holy City is identified as Jesus' bride, not his mother.

Once again our attention is drawn to the line from the Song of Songs: "I am a wall and my breasts are towers" (Song of Songs 8:10). The bride in the ancient liturgical poem describes herself using the metaphor of the Holy City—its twin watchtowers and its wall. Perhaps

*Fig. 7.1. Castles and towers are common watermarks found in paper
manufactured in Europe between 1280 and 1600.*

we can understand better how the Twin Towers in New York City represented the land and the people of the realm, and yes, of the world—as the symbol representing the *citadel,* or City of God. The blow struck on September 11, 2001, was a blow against the civilization built on Judeo-Christian foundations and against the millennial vision of humanity as a single human family, the one bride and partner of God.

In the window of the Dervaig Kilmore showing Christ embracing his bride, Mary is robed in a green gown and is obviously pregnant, just as the ekklesia—the Church as bride—is always symbolically pregnant. She is the sacred container or vessel filled with God, always expectant, always fruitful. But the mystical marriage that is the goal of history need not exclude the historical union of the beloveds who modeled that union: As above, so below!

The full meaning of the Incarnation is that divinity dwells in humanity, consecrating it by uniting with it, incarnating in and with and through matter.

This elevates the flesh and blood of humanity to a status equivalent to the holy partner of God, not separate but one with the creator. The Christ couple provides us with a beautiful mandala and vision of that intimate union—allowing us to image the Divine as partners.

An inscription appears in the window under the image of the Sacred Bridegroom and his bride. It reads: "Mary has chosen that good part which shall not be taken away from her" (Luke 10:42). This quotation identifies the bride in the window as Mary of Bethany who sat at the feet of Jesus, absorbed in his teachings. But she is also the woman who performed the nuptial anointing of Jesus at the banquet (John 12:3), thereby proclaiming the kingship of the Davidic Messiah and at the same time prophesying his imminent death.

The artist who created the stained-glass window at the Saint Mary's Church in Dervaig was a contemporary of Francis Thompson (1849–1907), whose remarkably prophetic poem "The Lily of the King" appears before the introduction to this book. Francis Thompson was a deeply religious Catholic who failed medical school and ended his life poverty-stricken and destitute due to opium addiction. He is most renowned for his celebrated poem *The Hound of Heaven.* In *Lilium Regis,* his vision of the Lily/Bride of Jesus being restored to her place of honor is deeply prophetic, for long has been the hour of her "unqueening." The bride in the poem represents the people, the ekklesia abandoned and devalued, called "most sorrowful of daughters." The promise is that her bridegroom will return for her: "His feet are coming to thee on the waters." The Kilmore artisan apparently shared this vision of the bride restored and crowned, a theme perhaps ignited into consciousness by the Pre-Raphaelite movement a generation or two earlier. The Christ couple in the 1906 window wears medieval garb similar to that worn by figures portrayed in numerous neo-romantic Grail paintings by that brotherhood of artists, attesting to a continued fascination with the lore of the Middle Ages.

What does the stained-glass image depicting the nuptials of Christ and Mary Magdalene of Bethany actually prove? It does not prove that Jesus was married. Given that there is no wedding license for Jesus and his bride, documented proof of their marriage remains elusive according to literalists who wish to be called historians. But the picture in the window does prove that the artist who created the window, drawing from deep wells of Christian scripture and tradition, was inspired to believe in the sacred marriage of Christ with the sister of Martha and

Lazarus, the bride whom nineteen hundred years of Christian tradition have called the Magdalene. The artisan chose to portray Jesus and Mary as hand-fasted, understanding Mary to be the woman who personified the Church assembly, the ekklesia, as the New Jerusalem. Prophecy found in the Book of Revelation provided him with a strong intuition that the ultimate purpose of Christian theology is the hieros gamos—the sacred union—or, perhaps better stated, the sacred *reunion,* of the Lamb and his bride, for do not be misled: The mandala at the heart of Christianity was—at its inception—the sacred partnership of the beloveds: "And I saw the Holy City, New Jerusalem, coming down out of heaven from God, made ready as a bride adorned for her husband" (Revelation 21:2).

Who can this woman be, other than the Daughter of Sion who represents her land and people. Surely it is not the Mother of Jesus, but instead his wife who belongs with him in the bridal chamber of our hearts and in the eternal throne room in heaven. More and more I am convinced that the sacred marriage was the stone (the *lapsit exillis*) that the builders rejected, which must be set as the cornerstone if the true temple is ever to be erected on the soil of planet Earth, just as it must be honored at the core of the human psyche. The eternal partnership of flesh and divinity, of male and female, and of all the polarities—is summed up in the mandala of the archetypal bride and bridegroom. Like the elusive reign of God, it is already in our midst.

The Reign of God

Based on evidence coded into the gospels themselves, the revealed paradigm for the kingdom or "reign of God" was sacred partnership. The proof for this assertion is evident in the Greek gematria for the mustard seed that expresses the harmonious union of masculine and feminine energies.[6]

This argument from the Greek texts of the gospels is virtually ignored by the guardians of the status quo. One conservative Catholic priest told me several years ago that he could not consider gematria valid evidence of the sacred marriage because it is Jewish. He made this comment even after I explained to him that symbolic numbers are not encoded by gematria only in the Hebrew Bible but also throughout the Greek New Testament. Like the proverbial ostrich, this ordained minister was prejudiced against the evidence and refused even to examine it. Because no religious authority had suggested he consider gematria in the gospels, he closed his mind to the possibility that he was not fully informed. To construct my theory, I returned to the original Greek of Christian scripture documents to demonstrate the historical practice of this literary device by the authors of sacred texts of the Christian canon.[7] The results are an astonishing testament to the union of the archetypal bride and bridegroom—styled as Lord and Lady of the Fishes.

The vital union of the opposite energies of the life force is a model for life on our planet, manifested in the intricate balance of all the workings of the universe—the cosmic dance. A significant parable attributed to Jesus bears testimony to this theme of sacred union at the core of the Christian message: "The reign of God is like a king who held a wedding banquet for his son" (Matthew 22:1). Many invited guests begged to be excused. This parable appears to be a midrash, or interpretation, of what actually transpired in the Roman province of Judaea in the first century: Jesus was inspired to teach and to celebrate a new model of radical gender equality and inclusiveness within his close circle of friends, lifting up the fallen feminine consciousness in the person of Mary Magdalene and embracing her fully, and at all levels. I envision them holding hands in her walled garden at Bethany on moonlit evenings in that last fatal springtime. But sadly, then as now, the guardians of the walls—entrenched in traditions of male dominance and patriarchal authority—were unable to hear his healing message of compassion and forgiveness, of justice and mercy, of gender equality and nonjudgmental inclusion. Apparently only the fringe or marginalized—prostitutes and tax collectors, simple peasants and day laborers, the blind, the lame, the halt, and mothers-in-law—were drawn to the inclusive promise of the reign of God revealed to be "already among us" and "in our midst."

In the aftermath of the Crucifixion, the bride of Jesus was removed to a place of safety to await the fulfillment of time, the time prophesied in Micah 4:10 when she will be rescued and her former dominion restored. Citizens of the Roman Empire in the first century were unwilling or unable to embrace the revolutionary message of Jesus: Love your enemies and your neighbor as yourself, serve one another generously, forgive infinitely, love unconditionally. Over the next several generations, the voice of the bride was silenced and the original egalitarian message of Jesus was hijacked by patriarchal interests, later to become entrenched in the heir apparent of the Roman Empire—the Vatican and its Pontifex Maximus, a title once borne by the Roman emperor—with tragic repercussions for the planet that are sadly not over yet. What we sow, we reap. And what was sown in the second and third centuries of the first Christian millennium was a civilization organized on the Logos/hierarchical model—the pyramid—which has inherent at its core the principles of fire *(pyr)* and power, both words stemming from the same root associated with "father energy." We should not be surprised that this model is exploding all around us— like bombs bursting in air!—because a civilization established on this model is out of balance. The attempt of Jesus to heal this separation was repudiated when the architects of Christianity rejected the cornerstone of his mission—the hieros gamos—and forced his beloved feminine counterpart into exile.

The vital question now is: Can we make this loss of the bride conscious—can we redeem the sacred feminine as partner—in time to save the planet we live on, our sacred vessel Earth, and the human family? Survival of the species *Homo sapiens* may depend upon the answer. It was not only her voice that was silenced when she was denigrated, devalued, and branded; it was our own!

What must we do to restore the voice of the bride?

Reclaiming the Sacred Union

The first step in restoring our Paradise Lost is to recognize that the mandala, or pattern of the Divine in holy partnership, is archetypal, manifested in ancient times as the sacred marriage of male and female— the interplay of cosmic forces in harmonious embrace. The harmonious interrelationship of the opposite energies was celebrated by our very earliest ancestors, who noted the eternal cycles of the seasons—the recurring cycles of life, death, and renewal. In their festivals, they celebrated the never-ending story of the return of the light at the winter solstice and the revitalization of the life force during the vernal equinox, in rites of hieros gamos, retained in the Easter mysteries named rather appropriately for the goddess Oester, whose name is derived from Ishtar, the consort of Tammuz. In recognizing this fundamental, archetypal paradigm for partnership, we affirm and embrace cosmic reality and experience at all levels.

But we must also acknowledge that religion is man-made and reflects our worldview and cosmology. In Pope John Paul II's suggestion during his 1999 Easter homily that the God on the ceiling of the Sistine Chapel was not really God—who is beyond all images—he was tacitly admitting that the image of God celebrated in Christian denominations worldwide is actually a false image of the Divine. Worship of an exclusively male image of God is idolatrous and has dangerous implications. It is dangerous not because it offends a passionate and jealous God, but because the masculine principle embodied in an exclusively masculine image of God becomes concretized on earth as a preference for males: for male children at birth and for male attitudes, wants, and desires. The trend of society is to become action-oriented, left-brained, and right-handed; everyone serves the power principle, everyone "rides the Beast." The waters of the artistic-intuitive are dammed and the rivers of living water—inspiration and mysticism—run dry. The garden becomes a wasteland.

Pope John Paul II once stated frankly that the Roman Catholic Church is not a democracy. How could it be, when its fathers silenced the voice of the bride in the second and third centuries and continued to disenfranchise subsequent generations, styling adherents as children rather than cocreators? But always in tension with the institution's hierarchy is the gospel itself, and the authentic, liberating teachings of Jesus Christ, in whom as Paul says "there is neither Jew nor Greek, slave nor free, male nor female, for all are one in Christ Jesus" (Galatians 3:28). Democracy is modeled on the ancient symbol of hieros gamos, the ✡. In this archetypal hexagram, the Δ, representing the hierarchical or masculine principle embodied in the three branches of elected government, is in intimate equilibrium with the ∇, representing the feminine—the will and voice of the people. A number of the founding fathers of the United States were, after all, Freemasons who had inherited enlightened traditions from the underground stream of European civilization.

The Healing of the Nations

Often I am asked, "What is the bottom line?"—what is my conclusion after thirty years devoted to restoring the bride to Christian consciousness? My answer is this: If the historical Jewish itinerant rabbi Jesus wasn't married, he should have been. Extensive evidence in the gospels themselves confirms his marriage on the literal/historical and physical plane because marriage was a fundamental obligation in Judaism, rarely waived without comment. His wife is clearly identified in the gospels—by virtue of her anointing of the messianic king at the banquet and their embrace at the garden tomb. But the answer to this question is far more important on the metaphysical plane: Imaging a celibate God is bound *(in extremis)* to create a dysfunctional family. In Christianity, the model for true partnership and equality has been too long denied, the bride stripped of her robes and exiled, her voice stolen, and in her place her mother-in-law elevated to a celestial throne at her son's right hand. Numerous medieval paintings celebrating this doctrine of the Roman Church show Jesus crowning his mother while Mary Magdalene kneels at their feet, still clasping the archetypal symbol of the nuptial anointing—the alabaster jar. And our fairy tales—*Snow White, Cinderella, Sleeping Beauty, The Little Mermaid*—show us the sinister face of the witch or stepmother who has stolen the birthright and exalted destiny of the true daughter/bride.

Apparently the ancient Greeks were already aware of the two hemispheres of the brain and their separate functions. The wasteland created by worship of a celibate male deity stripped of his feminine counterpart is an issue explored by medieval alchemists, whose principle of psychological integration is expressed in a series of woodcuts

Fig. 7.2. From a famous series of twenty woodcuts first printed in the second volume of De Alchimia opuscula complura veterum philosophorum, *Frankfurt 1550, that depicts the alchemical marriage of* sol *and* luna.

showing the masculine and feminine principles in proper relationship. In the sixteenth-century series *Rosary of the Philosophers,* the sacred union of the opposite principles is personified in a king and queen representing right and left hands, correlated to left-brain (Logos-reason) and right-brain (Eros-relatedness) interaction.

The woodcut series culminates in the marriage of the two figures and their final merging into one androgynous person, explained by Carl Jung's principle of the desired integration of Logos and Eros in each individual—the ultimate goal of enlightenment gleaned from life's experiences. Seeking God within the covers of a book is futile. True wisdom is more than intellect, more than experience. It flows from the union and integration of both ways of knowing—logic and intuition.

What are the possible benefits of restoring Mary Magdalene to her former position of highest honor? As bearer of the goddess archetype, the personification of the feminine face of reality, she brings us great gifts of creativity and intuitive knowing through experience. She also brings us profound connections with the earth and with one another—the kinship of all that lives and of all creation. The divine feminine is inclusive and tolerant, accepting of a wide diversity. She encourages us to live authentically and to connect with our emotions—with passion and compassion, with sensitivity to the needs of others, with consideration of their desires, even with willingness to listen (that rarest of all gifts!) and to relate to others in a way that comes from the heart. In a society that is deeply dualistic, we are becoming aware that stereotypes are dangerous and destructive: Teaching our sons not to cry and discouraging our daughters from studying math are grievous restraints on the human psyche. Gradually, we are grasping the meaning of Carl Jung's psychological research confirming that all of us are both male and female, "formed in the image of God," and that each of us must make her own—hopefully informed—choices at the core of her being. Stereotyping by gender and indoctrinating by memorized catechism do not feed the soul.

Having sent Mary Magdalene, the archetypal bearer of the color red and its connections to the flesh and blood of the human condition, into the obscurity of exile, Christian fathers deliberately dissociated themselves from the earth and the flesh. But in keeping with the important principle that what is suppressed becomes destructive, Western society is ever more materialistic and dissociated from the true feminine—agape, or unconditional love—expressed in deep wellsprings of mysticism and compassionate relationship with others. These elements were originally at the spiritual core of the gospel.

In our times, a tremendous surge of interest in the feminine half of creation has grown, manifested in women's studies programs in universities around the world, in welcoming women into government positions and into the clergy of some, though not all, Christian denominations. This impulse is evident, too, in renewed interest in spiritual paths of mysticism, service to others, and voluntary simplicity. But is there a growing willingness to listen? To be present to those who suffer? To console the grieving and to comfort the bereaved? To work for justice? These, too, are manifestations of the sacred feminine—the eros of God. The word *magnanimous* has at its root *mag*, "great lady" or "great mother."

Gradually, over the last two generations, women's voices have grown stronger, and in some regions of the world, they are now heard for the first time in recorded memory. Women's grave concerns are considered seriously in the halls of power, not only in the Christian West, but also across the globe; protect our children, protect our earth. And the movement goes forward. In the last two decades, we have seen new democracies born in regions suppressed by brutal dictatorship for millennia. Also in recent decades, women seeking role models to whom they can look for guidance rediscovered the many faces of the Great Goddess of antiquity. She had many names: Isis, Demeter, Inanna, Athene, Kwan Yin, Kali—strange-sounding names to women whose native tongue was English.

Twenty-five years ago, I was saddened by the movement of many women away from Christian denominations into worship of foreign-sounding goddesses. I wondered how they could abandon their Christian roots, how they could wander so far from home. Instead of leaving the Church of our youth, my own group of close friends developed a deep devotion to the Virgin Mary and to her rosary, which we prayed often—even daily—to Our Lady. Several members of the Emmanuel community went on pilgrimages to her shrines at Fátima, Lourdes, and Medugorje. One day in prayer in my own living room, I received the revelation that changed my life in an instant—that the preeminent woman in the Christian gospels was Mary Magdalene, bearer of the archetype of the goddesses of love, fertility, compassion, and wisdom. Somehow her story had been distorted and her exalted position denied. It was time to restore her to consciousness—not as a mere disciple or apostle of the historical rabbi Jesus, but as his beloved counterpart and complement—his wife.

Taking seriously this momentous revelation, and believing it to be a precious gift for the Church and for the entire human family, I devoted my life to researching the textual record and traditions and to correcting teachings regarding Mary Magdalene, never dreaming that time was ripening for a wider revelation of the restored paradigm I was shown. Now the good news of sacred partnership, embodied in the intimate union of Jesus and Mary Magdalene, is spreading across the planet like spontaneous combustion. Who could have anticipated this eventuality? Apparently the "sacred union" at the heart of the Christian mythology resonates with people on a very deep level.

Faced with the extraordinary phenomenon of Mary Magdalene's return, apologists for conservative Christianity are retrenching. Modern-day guardians of the walls, like the ones who attacked the bride in the Song of Songs and stripped her of her mantle, wish the bride would again disappear into oblivion. While clergy in some Christian denominations show a reluctant willingness to allow Mary Magdalene the role of an apostle—messenger of the resurrection—most are unwilling to consider the radical paradigm shift inherent in the sacred marriage. In defense of their inflexible position, some clergy claim that Jesus would have been too busy establishing his Church and preaching his message to bother with marriage—forgetting that marriage was a fundamental obligation of Jewish males. Others claim that the idea of sacred marriage is pagan, unwilling to admit it is the fundamental model for life on our planet—there is no other. Still others insist they are clinging to the tradition of Christianity that Jesus was both celibate and chaste—failing to understand that the hieros gamos was the original tradition of the earliest Christians and that the tradition to which they cling is a distortion of that original faith. Some Protestant denominations are apparently taking a second look at Roman Catholic doctrines of the Virgin Mary, showing a new willingness to give her special recognition as the Blessed Mother. Could this embrace of the Virgin Mary be an attempt to scuttle the far more radical suggestion that the favored Mary was the one called Magdalene and that, as the intimate companion and consort of Christ, it is *she* whom we need to embrace?

Might Jesus have been married? The answer is yes. Archbishop John Shelby Spong, the retired Episcopal archbishop of New Jersey, and Dr. William E. Phipps, a distinguished professor emeritus of religion and philosophy at David and Elkins College—both of whom have researched this subject in great depth—support the view that Jesus was very probably married. Nor are they alone. The evidence, although circumstantial, is powerful and undeniable. They and other clergy who have spoken on this issue, including Dr. Bart Ehrman, of the University of North Carolina, and Reverend Richard P. Mcbrien, of Notre Dame, have stated that they do not think acknowledging Jesus as married and a father would be in any way denigrating to him or harmful to Christian faith or doctrine. One of the basic tenets of the Church is that Jesus was fully human as well as divine, "like unto us in all things except sin." Marriage and sex within marriage are not sins. They are sacraments—signs of God's presence with us and of God's creative activity.

I raised other issues in my previous books that still need to be addressed. To my knowledge, critics rushing eagerly to debunk *The Da Vinci Code* have yet to offer a credible, rational rebuttal of the Greek gematria of the Magdalene (153) that associates her with the Great Goddess of antiquity and with the 153 fishes in the net (John 21:11), an acknowledged metaphor for the Church.[8] Some critics have snubbed the whole argument, dubbing it "numerology" and "New Age," believing that by giving gematria a negative spin, they can bury it. Gematria is not numerology. It is not New Age. It is a literary device used by educated philosophers of the Pythagorean tradition—both Jew and Greek—to enhance the meaning of important phrases in their texts. Because the phrases that contain gematria occur in the original Greek of the gospels, the argument that rests on the symbolic numbers in the New Testament stands as the most powerful original testimony to the sacred union—even now virtually ignored by most Bible scholars, including the seventy-four involved in the Jesus Seminar, who were apparently aware that gematria existed but decided not to examine it, although they spent many months establishing which quotes from the gospels were actually spoken by Jesus.[9] The symbolic numbers of the Greek canon have been embedded in the sacred texts of Christianity for two millennia. They are not going to go away. This might be the time to examine them to see what added insights they reveal about the original teachings of Jesus.[10]

The Whole Truth and Nothing But the Truth

In the aftermath of scandals involving Roman Catholic priests, people are now, for the first time in centuries, seriously asking, "What else did they forget to tell us?" Because the current crisis of confidence in the Catholic hierarchy is directly related to this hierarchy's dissociation from the sacred feminine, the relationship of Jesus and Mary Magdalene is entirely relevant to the problem. Enforced clerical celibacy, after centuries of devaluing the feminine half of creation, was mandated in 1139 when an edict by Pope Innocent II forced married priests to abandon their wives and children. Martin Luther, a former Roman Catholic priest, and other leaders of the Protestant Reformation, who saw no scriptural evidence for a celibate priesthood, repudiated mandatory celibacy when they established their own communities of believers. Luther himself married a former nun and had six children.

The twin pillars of my research are established in the canonical New Testament: The similarities between the Passion narratives with pagan rites celebrating the sacrificed king are indigenous to the gospels, as are the phrases coded by Greek gematria attesting to the preeminence of Mary Magdalene and to her unique partnership with Jesus. Each of these arguments from my research rests squarely in the accepted canon of our Judeo-Christian heritage. They are historical. They are not foreign or alien. They are not New Age. Nor are they dependent in any way on the gnostic gospels found in the Egyptian desert, texts declared heretical by Irenaeus in the second century and later anathematized by Athanasius of Alexandria in 367, although these texts do support the case that Mary Magdalene was the favorite companion whom Jesus cherished more than any other. The arguments made in my books in support of the hieros gamos union of Jesus and Mary Magdalene are rooted in the gospels. They are not fiction. They cannot be explained away or debunked. These points need to be taken seriously; they are rooted in the very scripture texts that all Christians believe to be the revealed and unerring Word of God.

The sacred union is confirmed in the earliest stratum of Christian witness, in the behavior of those brothers of Jesus and other apostles who, relying on the testimony of Paul in his first epistle to the

Corinthians, traveled as missionary couples with their sister-wives, spreading the good news of an egalitarian and inclusive reign of God modeled on the Song of Songs and the archetypal mandala for life itself. These earliest Christians acknowledged the kingdom already in our midst and spread out all around us, waiting for us to recognize, embrace, and celebrate the sacred union inherent in the mustard seed. Ultimately, that union is manifested in the partnership of Divinity and humanity, expressed in Paul's epistle: "Do you not know that your body is a temple for the Holy Spirit" (1 Corinthians 3:16). The core of the gospel message was attitude adjustment. We are each containers of an immanent and indwelling God. This is not the God on the ceiling of the Sistine Chapel, but the infinite, invisible, and ineffable Emmanuel who is "with us"—incarnate not only in Christ, but in us as well. The ultimate extension of this truth is demonstrated in physics by wave and particle theory—the manifest and the unmanifested are one, warp and woof of the same fabulous tapestry: existence itself.

I think it is likely that Jesus recognized and fully understood that his message would not be accepted immediately. As in the bridegroom parable mentioned earlier, the guests who were invited to the wedding feast of the king's son offered excuses and did not want to attend. The wedding feast implies the presence of the bride as well as the bridegroom. But the time of the reign of God was not yet. Jesus sowed the seeds of his kingdom, the mustard seed found in his parables and logia, and some seed fell on good ground. It strikes us as odd that Jesus chose the lowly mustard seed for his parable, because mustard is considered a noxious weed in the land where he preached it as a simile for the kingdom of heaven. It is scorned as of negligible value, yet its sum by gematria bears the symbolic sacred number of the marriage of masculine and feminine energies—1746.[11]

Bringing Water to the Wasteland

Eager to embrace the partnership paradigm, men and women from all over the globe are now opening their hearts and minds to Mary Magdalene, rereading her story and seeking her truth. Many who abandoned Christianity in tears a generation ago are returning, like the exiles in the sixth century B.C. returning from Babylon to the Holy City "bearing their sheaves." There is new hope in their hearts; they sense change on the wind, the prophetic breath of the Spirit: "[I]n the cities . . . there shall yet be heard, the cry of joy, the cry of gladness, the voice of the bridegroom, the voice of the bride . . ." (Jeremiah 33:10–11).

Due to the miraculous Internet, connecting people all over the world in nanoseconds, I receive amazing e-mails supporting my work and affirming my research. Often I receive poetry or works of art created to honor and celebrate Mary Magdalene. One such work (plate 22) is Jonathan Weber's (Williams, Oregon) painting of an irresistible vision of Mary Magdalene. Another (plate 23) is an archetypal image of the sacred union as conceived by Patricia Ballantine, of Phoenix. The painting by the California artist Joan Beth Clair, called *Alive in Her* (plate 9), is yet another gift inspired by the Magdalene.

And these are only a shadow of all that will be manifested in memory of her in generations to come. On the cusp of the New Age now dawning, we are preparing for another Passover. We are called out of the symbolic Egypt of our materialistic illusions and the selfish indulgence of our sensual appetites into the Promised Land of enlightenment, with its attendant gifts of reconciliation, inclusiveness, and partnership. We are called to embrace the Wisdom traditions of the ancestors—to incubate, to intuit, to dream, as suggested in Peter Kingsley's acclaimed book, *In the Dark Places of Wisdom*. As we leave the old paradigm of masculine dominance and patriarchal hegemony, passing over into the Age to Come, we must obey the request of Jesus to follow the man carrying a pitcher of water (Mark 14:13). He is the water carrier Aquarius—the zodiac sign of the next two-thousand-year stage of the journey on which the human family has embarked.

As we cross the river that is the final boundary, we cherish the sign of the age we are leaving, which we carry now crystallized in our hearts—the zodiac sign of the fishes—not one fish only, but two. The avatars, Lord and Lady of the Fishes, are hand-fasted in our new consciousness as in the window of Saint Mary's on the Isle of Mull (see plate 21). The final book of the Bible, the Apocalypse of John (Revelation), speaks of the river of the water of life flowing from the throne of God and the Lamb, nourishing the tree of life that bears twelve fruits and leaves for the healing of the nations (Revelation 22:2). When the Lamb is united with his bride, New Jerusalem, this river will flow through the Holy City and out into the desert. The trumpets are blowing. It is the end of the age and time for the nuptials of the Lamb.[12] In accepting at last the two-thousand-year-old invitation to attend the wedding feast of the king's son, we are now ready to welcome the bride as well, for inherent in our embrace of the bride is the healing of the nations:

> *For Sion's sake I will not be silent*
> *until her vindication shines forth like the dawn. . . .*
> *No longer shall she be called "abandoned"*
> *or her lands "desolate,"*
> *but she shall be called "beloved,"*
> *and her lands "espoused."*
>
> ISAIAH 62:1, 4

Epilogue

Who do you say that I am?

MATTHEW 16:15

When Jesus asked his disciples, "Who do men say that the son of man is?" (Matthew 16:13), they replied variously that some people thought Jesus was John the Baptist; others claimed he was Elijah or Jeremiah or one of the other prophets. Then Jesus queried them further, "Who do you say that I am?" And Simon-Peter replied, "You are the Christ, the Son of the Living God" (Matthew 16:16).

There were obviously many varying views about Jesus even in his own time, and there are many still. Some people see Jesus as a historical figure, a Galilean rabbi with a staff in his hand, an itinerant preacher and healer. Some see him as a cultural revolutionary, even a Zealot or an Essene. Finding negligible evidence for Jesus as a historical figure, others think he was the composite of many myths of the son-god tortured and sacrificed at the vernal equinox—an Adonis, Ba'al or Tammuz, Dionysus or Osiris.[1]

In this volume, we have examined a variety of views about Mary Magdalene, both traditional and heterodox, expressed in art and lore over Christianity's two millennia, as well as her connection to a number of powerful myths from the ancient world. In depth, we examined the most ancient tradition of the Church—that the title h Magdalene was given to Mary, the sister of Lazarus, not referring to a town destroyed for its immorality, but as a title of great honor and prophetic significance. And we have contemplated her presence in art, artifact, and folklore.

We have examined also the record of the historical Mary Magdalene, who allegedly witnessed the resurrection of the Savior and was sent to tell the good news to the other disciples and to the brothers of Jesus. And we have visited the legends and myths of the bride of the sacred king sent into exile to protect her from the dangerous talons of the malevolent dragon.

And who do people say that *she* is? Was she an actual historical person? A disciple of Jesus shod in sandals? A wealthy patroness? Perhaps a princess in her own right? Or was she a whore? Or even, as the gnostics taught, a mythic incarnation of the Holy Sophia? Was she the soul-sister and spouse of Jesus in a union similar to that of Tammuz and Ishtar or of Isis and Osiris? Or was she perhaps a sacred prostitute, a priestess representative of the Goddess? Was she a redheaded peasant? A frenzied demoniac? A favored daughter of Benjaminite lineage? Was she, like Wisdom herself, both scorned and beloved? Could she have been a wife and a mother? How can we know which face is hers, when no one has lifted her veil?

In these pages, we have examined her story from many angles. We have contemplated the sparse passages from the scriptures that speak of her and the many traditions that are spun around her. We have contemplated her images, mourned her loss, and begun to open our hearts and minds to her return to our consciousness.

The struggle to reclaim the real Mary Magdalene remains fraught with danger. Will we—once again—refuse to recognize in her an incarnation of the Divine, the other face of God? An important question remains to be answered: What position will the Mary called the Tower occupy when she is reinstated—as she must be—in the celestial throne room in heaven and in our communal psyche on earth? Will she be honored as apostle or as Bride?

Will she be blessed and embraced as the historical counterpart of Peter?

Or of Christ?

Who do we say that she is?

One answer, that she was an apostle equal in status and authority to Peter, seems to satisfy many clergy and scholars of Christian denominations. The right-handed and orthodox affirm Magdalene as the Apostle to the Apostles—a title of considerable honor, although her role was apparently short-lived, given that she carried only one message to the brethren of Jesus on that first Easter morning, and that her testimony was not at first believed. Modern scholars seem content with their proofs that Mary was not a prostitute and with reclaiming for her a position of prestige and authority as the first witness and messenger of the resurrected Lord. It is a limited role.

But the other answer, confirmed by left-handed intuitives who see visions and dream dreams, asserts that Mary Magdalene was the bride so long exiled from our consciousness. This vision of the sacred reunion of the beloveds is not new. The image of the holy braiding of flesh and divinity was always at the heart of the gospel—God incarnate in flesh, both male and female. Reclaiming Mary as bride brings water to the desert, causing flowers to bloom, healing broken hearts, setting prisoners free.

Notes

Introduction   *Mary Magdalene: Woman or Archetype?*

1. This and subsequent quotes in this paragraph are from "Letter of His Holiness Pope John Paul II to Artists," April 4, 1999, www.cin. org/jp2/jp2artist.html.

Chapter 1   *Mary, Mary*

1. *St. John's Missal for Every Day* (Belgium: Brepols' Catholic Press, 1958), 1314.

2. John W. Taylor, *The Coming of the Saints* (Thousand Oaks, Calif: Artisan Sales, 1985), 37.

3. See Morton Smith, *Jesus, the Magician* (San Francisco: Harper and Row, 1978), for a more complete discussion of contemporary sources related to demonic possession.

4. See Ann Graham Brock, *Mary Magdalene. The First Apostle: The Struggle for Authority* (Cambridge: Harvard University Press, 2002).

5. S. G. F. Brandon, *Jesus and the Zealots* (New York: Charles Scribner's Sons, 1967). Brandon presents the political scenario and reasons for downplaying the influence of the family of Jesus and his Jewish connections.

6. Morton Smith, *The Secret Gospel* (New York: Harper and Row, 1973). A copy of a letter quoting an apparently authentic version of Mark's gospel was discovered in 1958 by Dr. Smith at the Monastery of Mar Saba. The text of Clement of Alexandria's letter is available online.

7. Marvin W. Meyer, ed., *The Ancient Mysteries: A Sourcebook of Sacred Texts* (Philadelphia: University of Pennsylvania Press, 1999), 232. First published by Harper Collins, 1987.

8. See Margaret Starbird, *Magdalene's Lost Legacy* (Rochester, Vt.: Bear & Company, 2003), for explanation of the gematria and sacred geometry associated with Mary and especially with the epithet *h Magdalhnh*. The coded numbers provide direct association with the Great Goddess of the ancients and with Pythagorean geometry.

9. Jean-Yves LeLoup, *Gospel of Philip* (Rochester, Vt.: Inner Traditions, 2004), 65.

Chapter 2   Apostle to the Apostles

1. "The Lost Gospel of Peter," in *The Lost Books of the Bible and the Forgotten Books of Eden* (Cleveland: Forum Books, 1963).

2. This research is available on the Internet in a dissertation entitled "Mary Magdalene: Author of the Fourth Gospel," by Ramon K. Jusino, http://members.tripod.com/~Ramon_K_Jusino/magdalene.html.

3. See Dr. Dorothy Irvin's research published in her 2004 calendar, "The Archaeology of Women's Traditional Ministries in the Church, 300–1500 A.D." (St. Paul, Minn.: n.p., 2004).

Chapter 3   Bride and Beloved

1. *Saint John's Missal for Every Day*, 1315–16.

2. See Starbird, *The Woman with the Alabaster Jar*, 94–95, 123–24, 128, for details about the use of the letter X in medieval art as a symbol for esoteric or alternative Christianity and the Church of Amor.

3. Hugh Pope, "Mary Magdalene," in *The Catholic Encyclopedia,* vol. 9 (New York: Robert Appleton Company, 1910).

4. Pope John Paul II, *Rise, Let Us Be On Our Way* (New York: Warner Books, 2004), 33.

5. For examples of liturgical poetry celebrating the sacred marriage, see Samuel N. Kramer, *The Sacred Marriage Rite* (Bloomington: University of Indiana Press, 1969).

6. Michael Jordan, *Mary, the Unauthorized Biography* (London: Weidenfeld and Nicolson, 2001), 38–40.

7. James Teackle Dennis, trans., *The Burden of Isis* (London: John Murray, 1920), 34. Available online at www.sacred-texts.com/egy/boi/boi00.htm. This earlier liturgical poem from the cult of Isis and

Osiris contains many lines similar to, and some verbatim with, the Song of Songs, suggesting that the Song of Songs is a redaction and reworking of the earlier Egyptian liturgy celebrating solar and lunar divinities as bull and cow.

8. Karen King, *The Gospel of Mary of Magdala* (Santa Rosa, Calif.: Polebridge Press, 2003), 141. The title of this book is an interpolation of the title of the original text. Neither Magdala nor the title Magdalene is mentioned in the treatise or in its title. The text is called simply the Gospel of Mary.

9. Ibid., 151–52.

10. Frederic Manns, "Magdala dans les sources littéraires," in Studia Hierosolymitana. I Studi Archeologici, Studium Biblicum Franciscanum Collectio Maior 22 (1976): 311.

11. Yohanan Aharoni, et al., *The Macmillan Bible Atlas* (New York: Macmillan, 1968), 186.

12. Flavius Josephus, *The Jewish War*, book 3, chapter 10 (New York: Penguin, 1960). Available online at www.reluctant-messenger.com/josephusW03.htm.

13. Manns, "Magdala dans les sources littéraires," 312. See also Bruce Chilton and Craig Evans, eds., *Studying the Historical Jesus: Evaluations of the State of Current Research* (Leiden: E. J. Brill, 1994), 110.

14. Manns, 318.

15. Ibid., 326.

16. John W. Taylor, *The Coming of the Saints*, 36.

17. Ibid., 81.

18. *The Holy Bible: New International Version* (New York: The American Bible Society, 1978).

19. *The New American Bible for Catholics* (Nashville: Thomas Nelson Publishers, 1987).

20. T. Maraoka, *Emphatic Words and Structures in Biblical Hebrew* (Jerusalem: E. J. Brill, 1983), 138. "The primary function of *hnh*," according to Muraoka, "lies in indicating that the speaker or the writer wants to draw special attention . . . to a fact or object which can be said to be important, new, unexpected, and so forth."

Quoted in "The Function of *hnh* in the Syntax of Isaiah 8:18: A Study of *hnh* in Application to a Critical Question" by John David Duke Jr. See online at http://cv.nachmu.com/Function.html.

21. Caitlín Matthews, *Sophia, Goddess of Wisdom* (London: Aquarian Press, 1992), 81–82.

22. See Starbird, *Magdalene's Lost Legacy* for a more complete discussion of gematria related to Mary Magdalene, the number 153, and the sacred feminine among the ancients.

23. John Michell, *The Dimensions of Paradise* (San Francisco: Harper and Row, 1990), 193–95.

Chapter 4   Sophia, Spouse of the Lord

1. Leloup, *Gospel of Philip*, 3.

2. Christian scripture gematria is the subject of *Magdalene's Lost Legacy*. Numerous authors have written on this subject, all virtually ignored in the mainstream. Notable among the available studies of gematria are works by John Michell, David Fideler, Gordon Strachan, Robert Lawlor, Nigel Pennick, and Keith Critchlow.

3. Jean-Yves Leloup, *The Gospel of Mary Magdalene* (Rochester, Vt.: Inner Traditions, 2002), 171.

4. Leloup, *Gospel of Philip*, 65. For discussion of the translation of the word *koinōnos* (consort) with sexual connotations, see R. McL. Wilson, *The Gospel of Philip* (New York: Harper and Row, 1962), 35.

5. Leloup, *Gospel of Mary Magdalene*, 39.

6. Ibid., 37.

7. Ibid., *Gospel of Philip*, 3.

8. Ibid., 121.

9. Ibid., 73.

10. Ibid., 3.

11. Ibid., 11.

12. Ibid., 22.

13. Timothy Freke and Peter Gandy, *Jesus and the Lost Goddess: The*

Secret Teachings of the Original Christians (New York: Harmony
Books, 2001), 82–84.

14. Carl Schmidt, ed., "Pistis Sophia" in *Nag Hammadi Studies 9,* book
1, translated by Violet McDermott (Leiden: E. J. Brill, 1978), book
1, chapter 17. Text available online at www.webcom.com/~gnosis/
library/psoph.htm.

15. For associations of Mary Magdalene with the number 153, see
Starbird, *Magdalene's Lost Legacy,* 134–41. For discussion of the
geometry story problem in John 21, see David Fideler, *Jesus Christ,
Sun of God* (Wheaton, Ill.: Quest Books, 1993), 291–308.

16. Jonathan Hale, *The Old Way of Seeing* (Boston: Houghton Mifflin,
1994), 76–85.

Chapter 5   The Fragile Boat

1. Leloup, *The Gospel of Philip,* 65.

2. William E. Phipps, *The Sexuality of Jesus* (Cleveland, Ohio: Pilgrim
Press, 1996), 40. Phipps cites Kethuboth 63a and Sotah 4b.

3. Ibid. Phipps cites Ludwig Kohler, *Hebrew Man* (Nashville:
Abingdon Press, 1957), 89.

4. Donna B. Nielson, *Beloved Bridegroom* (**Phoenix:** Onyx Press,
1999), 168.

5. Edith Filliette, *Saint Mary Magdalene, Her Life and Times* (Newton
Falls, Mass.: Society of Saint Mary Magdalene, 1983) 137–39.

6. Ean Begg, *The Cult of the Black Virgin* (London: Penguin Books,
1985), 15.

7. See Starbird, *The Woman with the Alabaster Jar,* 59–62, for further
discussion of the legend of Sarah and the exiled Christians.

8. James Teackle Dennis, trans., *The Burden of Isis,* 34. Available
online at www.sacred-texts.com/egy/boi/boi00.htm.

9. Discussion of the Sangraal is found in Baigent, et al., *Holy Blood,
Holy Grail* (New York: Delacorte Press, 1982), 306, 359, 400. See also
Starbird, *The Woman with the Alabaster Jar,* 26–27; 50–52; 59–61.

10. Emma Jung and Marie-Louise von Franz, *The Grail Legend,* translated
by Andrea Dykes (London: Hodder and Stoughton, 1971). Jung and
von Franz suggest that the Grail legends circulated in an oral tradition

from the eighth or ninth century, a date similar to that given for early versions of Cinderella that spring up in many European languages.

11. See Starbird, *The Woman with the Alabaster Jar,* especially chapters 5–8, for detailed discussion of medieval art, artifacts, and fairy tales related to the heresy of the Holy Grail.

12. Charles-Moïse Briquet, *Les Filigranes: Dictionnaire historique des marques du papier dès leur apparition vers 1282 jusqu'en 1600* (Leipzig: n. p., 1923).

13. A drawing of this stone plate with the double-tailed mermaid is published in Margaret Starbird, *The Tarot Trumps and the Holy Grail* (Boulder, Colo.: WovenWord Press, 2000), 32.

14. Walter L. Wakefield and Austin P. Evans, *Heresies of the High Middle Ages* (New York: Columbia University Press, 1969), 238. Relevant chronicles of Ermengaud of Béziers and Pierre de Vaux-de-Cerney are quoted on pages 230–41. I am indebted to Sandra Hamblett for making me aware of this resource for heretical teachings in the Middle Ages.

15. Ibid., 234.

16. Martin Luther makes this comment in his *Table Talks.* Text is available online at http://ic.net/~erasmus/RAZ29.HTM.

17. Starbird, *Magdalene's Lost Legacy,* 138–41.

18. Ibid., *Alabaster Jar,* 94, 117–31, and especially 128–29.

Chapter 6   Desert Exile

1. Thomas Bulfinch, *Bulfinch's Mythology,* Modern Library Classics, www.mythology.com/orpheuseurydice.html.

2. David Fideler, *Jesus Christ, Sun of God,* 202, 351.

3. Ibid., 175.

4. Ibid., 352.

5. Gordan Strachan, *Jesus the Master Builder: Druid Mysteries and the Dawn of Christianity* (Edinburgh: Floris Books, 1998), 81–95. See also John Michell, *The Dimensions of Paradise,* 29–35, with reference to Stonehenge and its correspondence to the geometry of the New Jerusalem in the Book of Revelation.

6. Susan Haskins, *Mary Magdalen: Myth and Metaphor* (New York: Harcourt Brace, 1994), 65.

Chapter 7 The Beloved Espoused

1. Carl Jung, "Answer to Job," in R. F. C. Hull, trans., *The Portable Jung* (New York: Viking, 1971), 643.

2. Other images of Saint Barbara are displayed on the Internet, including a fifteenth-century wall painting in a church in the United Kingdom, online at www.paintedchurch.org/hessbarb.htm. Because long hair and a tower are icons distinctly associated with Mary Magdalene, this painting could easily be her image rather than that of Saint Barbara.

3. Pope John Paul II, 33.

4. See John Williamson, *The Oak King, the Holly King and the Unicorn* (New York: Harper and Row, 1986) for a thorough explanation of the symbolism of various plants and herbs in the unicorn tapestry panels at the Cloisters. A more complete discussion of the connection of the unicorn tapestries with the Song of Songs is found in Starbird, *The Woman with the Alabaster Jar,* 133–44.

5. See Starbird, *The Woman with the Alabaster Jar.* The medieval watermarks found in antique European Bibles show various symbolic twin towers, including the symbol currently used as the emblem for the U.S. Army Corps of Engineers, representing the ramparts of Jerusalem. The image also occurs in many medieval paintings that show the gate of Jerusalem flanked by two watchtowers, illustrated in figures 6.1 and 7.1, from Briquet, *Les Filigrans.*

6. Starbird, *Magdalene's Lost Legacy,* 57–59.

7. Ibid. The focus of the book is symbolic numbers in the New Testament and the revelations they encode by gematria. See also chapter 4, note 2.

8. Ibid., 135–41.

9. See *The Five Gospels: The Search for the Authentic Words of Jesus,* translated and with a commentary by Robert W. Funk, Roy W. Hoover, and the Jesus Seminar (New York: Polebridge Press, 1993).

10. See chapter 4, note 2.

11. Michell, *The Dimensions of Paradise,* 193–95.

12. For this prophetic insight concerning the imminent Nuptials of the Lamb, I am indebted to Mary T. Beben.

Epilogue

1. Alvin Boyd Kuhn, *A Rebirth for Christianity* (Wheaton, Ill.: Theosophical Publishing House, 2005). See also Freke and Gandy, *Jesus and the Lost Goddess* and *The Jesus Mysteries* for recent development of this thesis.

Chronology

B.C. (B.C.E.)

7000–3000	Neolithic period; god-goddess fertility cults are celebrated
2700–2200	Pyramids are built in Egypt
2000–1500	Megalithic monuments are raised; Stonehenge is built in England
1800–1600	Age of the Jewish patriarchs: Abraham, Isaac, Jacob, Joseph, and Joseph's eleven brothers
c. 1275–1250	Moses leads the Children of Israel out of Egypt and receives the Ten Commandments; Joshua conquers Canaan, the Holy Land
c. 1020–1002	King Saul rules Israel
c. 1002–962	King David rules Israel
c. 962–922	King Solomon rules an empire; builds the First Temple in Jerusalem
760–700	The Jewish prophets Isaiah, Hosea, Amos, and Micah live
650–560	The Jewish prophets Jeremiah and Ezekiel live
586	Nebuchadnezzar's armies conquer Jerusalem and destroy the Temple of Solomon
586–539	The Jewish people live in bondage in Babylon
580–500	Pythagoras develops the canon of symbolic numbers and establishes his school of philosophers and mathematicians
516	The Jewish people return to Jerusalem and begin to rebuild the city and the Temple

428–348	Plato is initiated into the secrets of priests and philosophers/mathematicians; he employs gematria in the *Timaeus* and *The Republic*
384–322	Aristotle, Greek scientist and philosopher of reason, lives
356–323	Macedonian Alexander the Great conquers an empire that stretches from Egypt to India
333–63	Greek hegemony is established over Palestine, Egypt, and the Near East; gematria is first used in Hebrew scriptures during the Hellenistic period
63	Roman general Pompey conquers Israel
44	Julius Caesar is assassinated
37–4	Reign of Herod the Great in Judaea; the Temple is rebuilt on a grand scale
c. 7–4	The birth of Jesus (exact date unknown)

A.D. (C.E.)

c. 28–29	The likely dates of the ministry of Jesus in Judaea and Galilee
c. 30–37	The crucifixion of Jesus (exact year unknown)
27–37	Pontius Pilate is procurator of Palestine
c. 35–38	Saul/Paul is converted on the road to Damascus
c. 42–44	A boat bearing the refugee family of Mary Magdalene arrives on the coast of Gaul
46–67	Paul travels and writes epistles to various Christian communities
c. 62–67	Acts of the Apostles is written, probably by Luke the Evangelist
65	Nero burns Rome; Peter and Paul are martyred in Rome
66–70	Jews revolt against Roman occupation of their land
67	Destruction of Taricheae by the Romans
c. 70–71	The Gospel of Mark is written, probably in Rome (the original is repressed)
67	The fall of Taricheae
70	The fall of Jerusalem; destruction of Herod's temple

73	The fall of the final Jewish stronghold at Masada
c. 80–85	The Gospel of Matthew is written
c. 85–90	The Gospel of Luke is written
c. 90–95	The Gospel of John is written
c. 95–105	The Apocalypse of John (Book of Revelation) is written
c. 100	The final (edited or censored?) canonical Gospel of Mark appears
120–300	The gnostic gospels are written
100–150	The Gospel of Mary (Greek and Coptic fragments) is written; the Gospel of Thomas is written (some parts may predate Mark)
150–200	The Gospel of Philip is written
c. 130–202	Bishop Irenaeus of Lyons, author of *Against Heresies*, castigates gnostics
c. 150	The earliest copy appears of Peshitta, the New Testament in Aramaic
c. 150	The Pre-Coptic Exile Carpet is created, probably by Christian gnostics in Egypt
155–220	Tertullian, a Christian father who becomes a heretic, forms his own order and writes a polemic against the gnostics and "numbers theology"
170–235	Hippolytus of Rome, a Christian Scripture exegete, writes a commentary on Song of Songs and a polemic against heretics
185–254	Origen, a brilliant Christian philosopher, of Alexandria, lives; he is condemned as a heretic at the Fifth Ecumenical Council in 553
c. 250–300	The Pistis Sophia and other gnostic treatises are written
325	The Council of Nicea is held
342–420	Jerome translates Greek scriptures into Latin, obscuring Greek gematria
c. 350	Earliest extant copies appear of the Greek New Testament (Sinaiticus, Vaticanus)
354–430	Augustine, bishop of Hippo, lives

c. 360–400	Gnostics are persecuted; gnostic gospels are hidden in earthen jars near Nag Hammadi
420–500	Barbarians sweep through the Roman Empire; Rome falls and the pope surrenders to Attila; the Roman Empire disintegrates
428–751	The Merovingian dynasty rules the kingdom of the Franks (Gaul)
481–511	King Clovis I converts the Franks to Roman Catholicism
591	In a homily, Pope Gregory the Great (540–604) declares Mary Magdalene to be identified with both the sister of Lazarus, who anoints Jesus, and the sinner in Luke's gospel
550–711	Muslim armies sweep across the Near East and Africa and conquer and occupy Spain and southern France
732	Charles Martel (d. 741) defeats the Moors at Poitiers, saving Christian Europe
500–1000	The Dark Ages commence; barbarian hordes and Viking raids threaten the vestiges of Roman civilization; monastic orders rise and preserve scholarship and Christian culture
800	Charlemagne is crowned Holy Roman Emperor by the pope in Rome
1066	Norman William the Conqueror conquers England
1098–99	First Crusade of Europeans conquers Jerusalem and triumphs over the Saracens
1118	Order of the Poor Knights of the Temple of Solomon is established
1139	Pope Innocent II demands priestly celibacy.
1209–1250	The pope and the French king conduct the brutal Albigensian Crusade against the heretics of the Languedoc
1224–1274	Thomas Aquinas lives; he dies while giving commentary on the Song of Songs
1233–1237	The Inquisition is established to eradicate heresies
1244	The fall of Montségur, citadel seminary of the Cathars

1291	Crusaders are expelled from the Near East; the Order of the Knights of the Temple is liquidated and its members are imprisoned and martyred
1380	The first English translation of the Bible appears, translated from the Latin Vulgate by John Wycliffe
c. 1456	Muslims conquer Constantinople; Greek Christians flee to Europe, bringing with them Greek texts from their libraries
1450s	The printing press is invented; translations of the Bible are printed in Mainz
1492	Columbus arrives in the West Indies
1500	The end of the Middle Ages and the beginning of the Renaissance
1516	Erasmus's Latin/Greek Bible is printed with corrections to the Vulgate
1517	Martin Luther nails his theses to the door of the church in Wittenberg, challenging the Vatican
1529	Martin Luther publishes his translation of the German Bible
1588	England defeats the Spanish Armada
1611	The King James Bible is published in English, translated from the Greek *Textus Receptus*
1848	Pre-Raphaelite Brotherhood founded by Dante Rossetti
1870	First Vatican Council declares doctrine of papal infallibility
1906	Stained-glass window created for Saint Mary's Church in Dervaig, Isle of Mull
1945	Codices of the gnostic library are discovered near Nag Hammadi, Egypt
1947	The Dead Sea Scrolls are discovered near the ruins of Qumran in Israel
1969	The liturgy for Mary Magdalene's feast is revised: Mention of both Lazarus and the Bride (Psalm 45) are deleted
1980	In commemoration of the discovery of her grave seven hundred years earlier, the feast day of Mary Magdalene is celebrated in Saint Maximin in Provence

Bibliography

Aharoni, Yohanan, et al. *The Macmillan Bible Atlas*. New York: Macmillan Publishing Company, 1968.

Baigent, Michael, Richard Leigh, and Henry Lincoln. *Holy Blood, Holy Grail*. New York: Delacorte Press, 1982.

Bayley, Harold. *The Lost Language of Symbolism*. 1912 reprint, Totowa, N.J.: Rowman and Littlefield, 1974.

Begg, Ean. *The Cult of the Black Virgin*. London: Penguin Books, 1985.

Bellevie, Lesa. "Brides in Exile: A Primordial Religious Impulse Latent in Western Civilization." www.magdalene.org/pagan_scholars_talk.

Borg, Marcus J. *Meeting Jesus Again for the First Time*. San Francisco: Harper Collins, 1995.

Brandon, S. G. F. *Jesus and the Zealots*. New York: Charles Scribner's Sons, 1967.

Briquet, Charles-Moïse. *Les Filigranes: Dictionnaire historique des marques du papier dès leur apparition vers 1282 jusqu'en 1600* (Leipzig: n.p., 1923)

Brock, Ann Graham. *Mary Magdalene. The First Apostle: The Struggle for Authority*. Cambridge: Harvard University Press, 2002.

Brown, Raymond E. *The Community of the Beloved Disciple*. New York: Paulist Press, 1979.

———, ed. *The Jerome Biblical Commentary*. New Jersey City, N.J.: Prentice Hall, 1968.

Bulfinch, Thomas. *Bulfinch's Mythology*. Modern Library Classics. www.mythology.com

Cartlidge, David R., and David L. Dungan, eds. *Documents for Study of the Gospels*. Philadelphia: Fortress Press, 1980.

Chilton, Bruce, and Craig Evans, eds. *Studying the Historical Jesus: Evaluations of the State of Current Research*. Leiden: E. J. Brill, 1994.

Cruden, Alexander. *Cruden's Unabridged Concordance*. Grand Rapids, Mich.: Baker Book House, 1973.

Daniélou, Jean. *The Dead Sea Scrolls and Primitive Christianity*. Translated by Salvator Attanasio. New York: New American Library, 1962.

Dennis, James Teackle, trans. *The Burden of Isis*. London: John Murray, 1920.

Duke, John David. "The Function of *hnh* in the Syntax of Isaiah 8:18: A Study of *hnh* in Application to a Critical Question." http:cv.nachmu.com/Function.html.

Eisler, Riane. *The Chalice and the Blade*. San Francisco: Harper and Row, 1988.

Fideler, David. *Jesus Christ, Sun of God*. Wheaton, Ill.: Quest Books, 1993.

Filliette, Edith. *Saint Mary Magdalene, Her Life and Times*. Newton Falls, Mass.: Society of Saint Mary Magdalene, 1983.

Franz, Marie-Louise von. *Alchemy*. Toronto: Inner City Books, 1980.

Frazier, Sir James George. *The Golden Bough: A Study in Magic and Religion*. New York: The Macmillan Company, 1951.

Freke, Timothy, and Peter Gandy. *Jesus and the Lost Goddess: the Secret Teachings of the Original Christians*. New York: Harmony Books, 2001.

———. *The Jesus Mysteries: Was the "Original Jesus" a Pagan God?* New York: Three Rivers Press, 1999.

Funk, Robert W., Roy W. Hoover, and the Jesus Seminar, eds. and trans. *The Five Gospels: The Search for the Authentic Words of Jesus*. New York: Polebridge Press, 1993.

Hale, Jonathan. *The Old Way of Seeing*. Boston: Houghton Mifflin, 1994.

Halliday, William R. *The Pagan Background of Early Christianity*. New York: Cooper Square Publishers, 1970.

Hamilton, Edith. *Mythology*. New York: New American Library, Mentor Books, 1969.

Haskins, Susan. *Mary Magdalene: Myth and Metaphor*. New York: Harcourt Brace, 1994.

Hulme, F. Edward. *Symbolism in Christian Art*. Detroit: Gale Research, 1969.

Inman, Thomas. *Ancient Pagan and Modern Christian Symbolism*. Williamstown, Mass: Corner House Publishers, 1978.

Jones, F. Stanley, ed. *Which Mary? Marys in the Early Christian Tradition*. SBL Symposium Series 20. Atlanta: Society of Biblical Literature, 2002.

Jordan, Michael. *Mary, the Unauthorized Biography*. London: Weidenfeld and Nicolson, 2001.

Josephus, Flavius. *The Jewish War*. New York: Penguin Classics, 1960.

Jung, Carl. *The Portable Jung*. Edited by Joseph Campbell. Translated by R. F. C. Hull. New York: Viking, 1971.

Jung, Emma, and Marie-Louise von Franz. *The Grail Legend*. Translated by Andrea Dykes. London: Hodder and Stoughton, 1971.

Jusino, Ramon K. "Mary Magdalene: Author of the Fourth Gospel." Treatise: www.BelovedDisciple.org.

King, Karen L. *The Gospel of Mary of Magdala: Jesus and the First Woman Apostle*. Santa Rosa, Calif.: Polebridge Press, 2003.

Kramer, Samuel N. *The Sacred Marriage Rite*. Bloomington: Indiana University Press, 1969

Leloup, Jean-Yves. *The Gospel of Mary Magdalene*. Rochester, Vt.: Inner Traditions, 2002.

———. *The Gospel of Philip*. Rochester, Vt.: Inner Traditions, 2004.

———. *The Gospel of Thomas*. Rochester, Vt.: Inner Traditions, 2005.

Lucas, Jerry, and Del Washburn. *Theomatics: God's Best Kept Secret Revealed*. New York: Stein and Day, 1977.

Luther, Martin. "Table Talk" in *Luther's Words, Luther's Works*. American edition, edited by Jaroslav Pelikan (vols. 1–30) and Helmut T. Lehmann (vols. 31–55). St. Louis: Concordia Publishing House (vols. 1–30); Philadelphia: Fortress Press (vols. 31–55), 1955.

Malvern, Marjorie M. *Venus in Sackcloth*. Edwardsville: Southern Illinois University Press, 1975.

Manns, Frederic. "Magdala dans les sources littéraires," Studia Hierosolymitana. I Studi Archeologici, Studium Biblicum Franciscanum Collectio Maior 22 (1976).

Maraoka, T. *Emphatic Words and Structures in Biblical Hebrew*. Jerusalem: E. J. Brill, 1983.

Matthews, Caitlín. *Sophia, Goddess of Wisdom*. London: Aquarian Press, 1992.

Michell, John. *The City of Revelation*. Reprint. New York: David McKay Company, 1972.

———. *The Dimensions of Paradise*. San Francisco: Harper and Row, 1990.

Nielson, Donna B. *Beloved Bridegroom*. Phoenix: Onyx Press, 1999.

Pagels, Elaine. *The Gnostic Gospels*. New York: Vintage, 1981.

Patai, Raphael. *The Hebrew Goddess*. Hoboken, N.J.: KTAV Publishing House, 1967.

Phipps, William E. *Was Jesus Married?* New York: Harper and Row, 1970.

———. *The Sexuality of Jesus.* Cleveland, Ohio: Pilgrim Press, 1996.

Pope, Hugh. "Mary Magdalene" in *The Catholic Encyclopedia,* vol. 9. New York: Robert Appleton Company, 1910.

Pope John Paul II. "Letter of His Holiness Pope John Paul II to Artists," April 4, 1999, www.cin.org/jp2/jp2artist.html.

———. *Rise, Let Us Be On Our Way.* New York: Warner Books, 2004.

Pope, Marvin H. *Song of Songs.* Anchor Bible Series. Garden City, N.Y.: Doubleday, 1983.

Qualls-Corbett, Nancy. *The Sacred Prostitute.* Toronto: Inner City Books, 1988.

Ranke-Heinemann, Uta. *Eunuchs for the Kingdom of Heaven: Women, Sexuality and the Catholic Church.* Translated by Peter Heinegg. New York: Doubleday, 1990.

Ringgren, Helmar. *Religions of the Ancient Near East.* Translated by John Sturdy. Philadelphia: Westminster Press, 1973.

Robinson, James M., ed. *The Nag Hammadi Library: In English.* San Francisco: Harper and Row, 1981.

Rougemont, Denis de. *Love in the Western World.* Translated by Montgomery Belgion. New York: Pantheon Books, 1956.

Schonfield, Hugh. *The Pentecost Revolution.* Dorset, England: Element Books, 1985.

Silberer, Herbert. *Hidden Symbolism of Alchemy and the Occult Arts.* 1917. Reprint. New York: Dover Publications, 1971.

Smith, Morton. *Jesus, the Magician.* San Francisco: Harper and Row, 1978.

———. *The Secret Gospel.* New York: Harper and Row, 1973.

Starbird, Margaret. *The Goddess in the Gospels: Reclaiming the Sacred Feminine.* Santa Fe: Bear & Company, 1998.

———. *Magdalene's Lost Legacy: Symbolic Numbers and the Sacred Union in Christianity.* Rochester, Vt.: Bear & Company, 2003.

———. *The Woman with the Alabaster Jar: Mary Magdalen and the Holy Grail.* Santa Fe: Bear & Company, 1993.

Strachan, Gordon. *Jesus the Master Builder: Druid Mysteries and the Dawn of Christianity.* Edinburgh: Floris Books, 1998.

St. John's Missal for Every Day. Belgium: Brepols' Catholic Press, 1958.

Stone, Merlin. *When God Was a Woman.* New York: Dial Press, 1976.

"The Lost Gospel of Peter" in *The Lost Books of the Bible and the Forgotten Books of Eden.* Cleveland: Forum Books, 1963.

Taylor, John W. *The Coming of the Saints*. Thousand Oaks, Calif.: Artisan Sales, 1985.

Vermes, G. *The Dead Sea Scrolls in English*. New York: Penguin Books, 1987.

Wakefield, Walter L., and Austin P. Evans. *Heresies of the High Middle Ages*. New York: Columbia University Press, 1969.

Williamson, John. *The Oak King, the Holly King and the Unicorn*. New York: Harper and Row, 1986.

Young, Wayland. *Eros Denied*. New York: Grove Press, 1964.

Bibles

New International Version. New York: The American Bible Society, 1978.

Joseph New Catholic Edition of the Holy Bible. New York: Catholic Book Publishing Co., 1963.

Revised Standard Edition. New York: Meridian, 1974.

The NKJV Greek English Interlinear New Testament. Translated by Arthur L. Farstad, Zane C. Hodges, C. Michael Moss, Robert E. Picirilli, Wilbur N. Pickering. Nashville: Thomas Nelson Publishers, 1994.

Web Sites

Alchemy
www.levity.com/alchemy

Early Christian Writings
www.earlychristianwritings.com
www.earlychristianwritings.com/text/josephus/josephus.htm

Gnostic Archive
www.gnosis.org/welcome.html
www.webcom.com/~gnosis/library/psoph.htm

Mary Magdalene
www.magdalene.org
www.beloveddisciple.org

Index

1 Corinthians, 50, 51, 79, 90, 151
1 John, 76
1 Timothy, 33, 86, 115

Acts of the Apostles, 32, 92. *See also*
    Book of Acts
Adam, 4, 12
Adam, Stephen, **plate 21**
Adonis, 49, 64, 154
agape, 30, 146
Age of Pisces, 105
Agraulos, 65
Agrippa II, 54
Ahasuerus, King, 121
Akiba, Rabbi, 43, 88
alabaster jar, 1, 9, 38, 40, 42, 44–46,
    59, 129, 130, 135, 144
Albigensian Crusade, 107, 108
Albright, 67
alchemists, 144
Alive in Her, 66, 152, **plate 9**
Ambrose, Saint 58
Amos, 63
Andrew, Saint, 31
anointing, 11, 14, 29, 40-50, 52, 56,
    59, 68, 74, 93, 96, 135, 139, 144
Answer to Job, 125
anthropos, 73
Apocalypse (of John), 125, 152. *See
    also* Revelation
Apocalypse of Peter, 84
Apollo, 78, 111
Aquarius, 152

Aquinas, Thomas, 58
Aramaic, 53–55, 57, 59–61, 63, 92,
    116, 127
Aristotle, 115
Artemis, 94
Asherah, 49, 119
Astarte, 49
Athanasius of Alexandria, 70, 150
Athena (Athene), 65–66, 147
Attis, 64
Augustine of Hippo, Saint 12, 58

Babylonian Talmud, 56–57
Ballantine, Patricia K., 152
barbara, 129
Barbara, 126–30
Bark of Mary, 93, 96
Bark of Peter, 93
Beast, 143
The Beloved, 132, **plate 17**
Beloved Disciple, 30
beloveds, 48, 52, 68, 73, 108, 110, 113,
    131, 134, 136, 138, 140, 156
Beltane, 135
Benjamin, 67, 96
Bernard, 58
Bethlehem, 8, 62, 67
Béziers, 107
Black Madonna, 117–18 123, 135
Blessed Mother, 21, 24, 28, 34, 61,
    82, 148
blue (color), 98, 100, 103, 108
Book of Acts, 86, 93, 132